PENGUIN

THE SECRET LIFE OF LASZ

John Bierman has written many books, of which the most recent is *Alamein: War Without Hate*, co-written with Colin Smith and published by Viking in 2002. Bierman, a seasoned ex-BBC television correspondent and documentary film-maker, worked as a senior sub-editor in Fleet Street and edited dailies in East Africa and the West Indies before moving to broadcasting.

The Secret Life of Laszlo Almasy

The Real English Patient

JOHN BIERMAN

PENGUIN BOOKS

PENGUIN BOOKS

Published by the Penguin Group
Penguin Books Ltd, 80 Strand, London WC2R 0RL, England
Penguin Group (USA) Inc., 375 Hudson Street, New York, New York 10014, USA
Penguin Group (Canada), 10 Alcorn Avenue, Toronto, Ontario, Canada M4V 3B2
(a division of Pearson Penguin Canada Inc.)
Penguin Ireland, 25 St Stephen's Green, Dublin 2, Ireland
(a division of Penguin Books Ltd)
Penguin Group (Australia), 250 Camberwell Road, Camberwell, Victoria 3124, Australia
(a division of Pearson Australia Group Pty Ltd)
Penguin Books India Pvt Ltd, 11 Community Centre, Panchsheel Park, New Delhi – 110 017, India
Penguin Group (NZ), cnr Airborne and Rosedale Roads, Albany, Auckland 1310, New Zealand
(a division of Pearson New Zealand Ltd)
Penguin Books (South Africa) (Pty) Ltd, 24 Sturdee Avenue, Rosebank 2196, South Africa

Penguin Books Ltd, Registered Offices: 80 Strand, London WC2R 0RL, England

www.penguin.com

First published by Viking 2004
Published in Penguin Books 2005
1

Copyright © John Bierman, 2004
All rights reserved

The moral right of the author has been asserted

Set by Rowland Phototypesetting Ltd, Bury St Edmunds, Suffolk
Printed in England by Clays Ltd, St Ives plc

In tribute to Ralph Bagnold, Bill Kennedy Shaw,
Pat Clayton and all the other stalwarts of
the Long Range Desert Group.

List of Illustrations

Illustration Acknowledgements

The authors and the publishers are grateful to the following for permission to reproduce the illustrations:

Vas Megyei Leveltar, Szombathely, Hungary: 1, 2, 3
Kurt Mayer: 4, 5
Royal Geographical Society: 6, 7, 11, 17, 18, 21, 22, 23
Peter Clayton: 8, 9, 10, 13, 14, 15, 24, 25, 26
Peter Steigerwald/Frobenius Institute, Frankfurt: 12, 16, 19
From Janos Kubassek, *A Szahara Buvoleteben*: 20, 31
Revista Militar, Italy: 27, 28

List of Illustrations

General map of the region showing the principal places visited
by Almasy during his desert travels

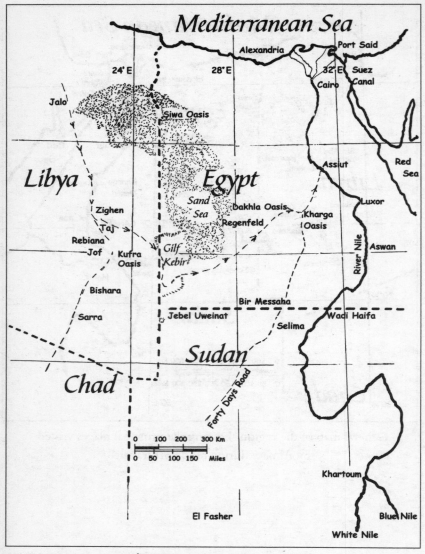

General map of the region: the arrowed lines show Almasy's
route from Jalo to Assiut during Operation Salam in 1942

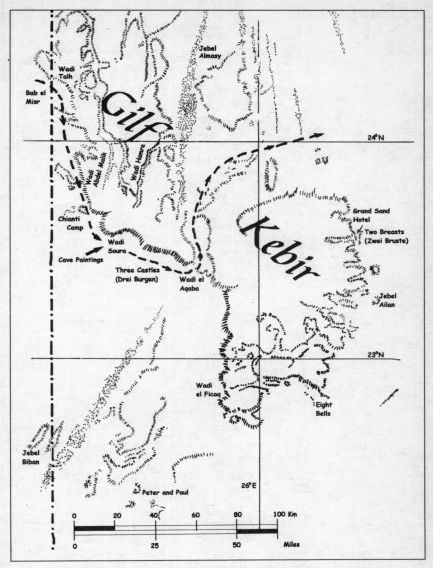

Gilf Kebir: the arrowed line indicates Almasy's Operation
Salam route alongside and through Gilf Kebir as he took the
two German spies to the Nile Valley

Prologue

In December 1950, just a couple of days after Christmas, King Farouk I (and last) of Egypt invited six hundred luminaries of the Western academic and scientific world – among them the vice-chancellors of Oxford and Cambridge and the presidents of the Royal Colleges of Physicians and Surgeons – to Cairo.

The ostensible purpose of this extravagant exercise in public relations was 'to discuss desert problems'. It was also to make formal announcement of the appointment of the Hungarian-born explorer, cartographer and aviator Laszlo Almasy as director of the newly established Cairo Desert Institute. Its undeclared but barely disguised purpose was to cock a snook at Great Britain.

For the best part of a century, Egypt had been little more than a vassal state of the British, its monarchs at best patronized and humiliated even when they toed the London line and at worst bullied and exiled when they did not. True, a 1936 treaty had given the Egyptians their 'independence', but in reality their quasi-colonial status had hardly changed, as Farouk learned to his eternal chagrin when, in February 1942, at the height of World War II, the British surrounded his palace with tanks and infantry, forcing him to the very brink of abdication* for the impertinence of showing reluctance to accept Britain's nominee as his prime minister.

So it no doubt gave Farouk no small measure of satisfaction to invite the cream of the British establishment to his capital some five years after the end of the war in order to flaunt his elevation of Almasy, an active enemy of Britain during the war, to head the Desert Institute named for Farouk's late father, King Fuad. The appointment, though prestigious, had actually been made nine months earlier and was, anyway, hardly of world-shaking import. For Farouk to go to such expense to introduce the new director to the world may have seemed a petty, almost childish, act of revenge, but it was about the only revenge available to him at the time.

By the age of thirty-two Farouk, once a slender, handsome youth and in many ways the poster boy of the Arab world, despite his mixed Albanian–Turkish–Greek descent, had become a corrupt and self-indulgent caricature of his former self, an obese and balding lecher with a vast personal fortune at his disposal but little on his mind save gambling, drinking, overeating, driving fast cars and bedding faster women. If anything else did preoccupy him it was his

* In July 1952, Farouk *was* forced to abdicate – not by the British but by his own army officers who sent him into luxurious European exile, where he died in 1965 as a citizen of Monaco. In this context, it is perhaps worth recalling that while gambling in Monte Carlo Farouk half-jokingly forecast that by the end of the twentieth century there would be only five kings left in the world: the kings of hearts, diamonds, clubs and spades and the King of England.

enduring resentment of the British, and in particular of his personal nemesis, the former British ambassador to Egypt, Sir Miles Lampson.

It was Lampson who had sent the tanks to surround the Abdin Palace when the young king – or 'the boy', as the ambassador used to call him, and not just in private – dared to oppose his will. Needless to say, Lampson was not on Farouk's 1950 invitation list. By that time he was retired and back in Britain, with a peerage as compensation for having been denied his life's ambition, the Viceroyship of India, by the subcontinent's accession to independence in 1947. But even though departed, Lampson's six-foot-five, 250-pound figure remained for Farouk the personification of the imperial domination he had laboured under since his coronation in 1936.

However puny it may seem as retaliation, Farouk's public relations spectacular was, in the words of retired British brigadier Ralph Bagnold, 'a fantastic occasion' in other respects. Bagnold knew Almasy from pre-war days when both belonged to the informal Zerzura Club of pioneering desert explorers sharing a common interest in finding the eponymous and legendary 'lost oasis of the little birds' in the North African desert.

In 1940, Bagnold had founded and led the Long Range Desert Group, perhaps the most dashing and effective of all the irregular formations deployed by the British in World War II. For his part, Almasy had gone to war as desert adviser to Germany's Field Marshal Erwin Rommel and to head a 'special commando' that might, but for Rommel's lack of interest, have hoped to rival Bagnold's LRDG.

Not surprisingly, then, Bagnold and Almasy eyed each other warily when they met again for the first time since the war at Farouk's Abdin Palace party. And what a party it was! A ninety-piece Arab musical ensemble, performing on traditional instruments, entertained Farouk's guests in the palace's five-hundred-seat theatre, followed by elaborate dance productions featuring an Indian and a Spanish *corps de ballet*. The palace itself, although situated in the middle of a central Cairo slum, was an imposing Italianate building boasting 550 rooms, a stunning alabaster entrance hall (decorated by life-sized mosaics of naked dancing girls), elaborate grounds tended by more than two hundred gardeners and a garage that could house two hundred cars. It was, said America's *Life* magazine, 'one of the world's most magnificent royal palaces'.

In his memoirs, Bagnold would recall that on each side of every stair, as Farouk's high-profile guests went up to dinner, stood a tall, black Nubian, 'stiff as a statue and carrying a spear'.

Against the whole of one wall were piled, ceiling high, an array of luscious dishes such as few of us had seen since before the war. Centre front rose a high dais on which stood a bowl of gold several feet in diameter. Behind it a great, grinning black Nubian in a red and gold gown ladled out drinks for us in gold goblets . . . I saw two vice-chancellors standing together in awe. One said to the other 'I just don't believe it.' Then we ate a buffet off solid gold plates.

By the time the palace party ended, relations between Bagnold and Almasy had warmed sufficiently for them to

– not so much about a given individual but about his or her character and the human condition in general – than the most rigorously researched, artfully constructed and factually faithful biography. A novelist can 'make things up', in the best sense of the phrase; a biographer cannot.

Insofar as Ondaatje's plot line controverts or ignores many of the essential facts about Almasy's life, and takes liberties with the time-scale of historic events, the novel and the film based on it are ahistorical; but the notion that it is amoral because it is apolitical is harder to sustain.

Objectors to the Hollywood version of *The English Patient*, such as the moral philosopher Thomas Hurka, have argued that an important ethical issue lies at the centre of the plot. The fictional Almasy put his personal desires above his higher obligation to combat the evil of Nazism and made a philosophically indefensible choice in striking a Faustian bargain with the Germans by trading his desert expertise for the use of an aircraft, enabling him to keep his promise to his dead lover and return to the cave where he had been forced to leave her.

It is this utter denigration of the political that makes *The English Patient* immoral [argues Professor Hurka]. There was not just some political end at stake in the Second World War; there was resistance to Nazism, a movement threatening millions of innocent people. Yet the movie treats even this end as morally inconsequential.

Elizabeth Salett, whose father was the Hungarian consul-general in pre-war Egypt, went further. Writing in the *Washington Post*, she took issue with the film's depiction of

Almasy as 'an accidental spy responding to personal tragedy'. Drawing on her father's recollections, she described Almasy as 'a committed Nazi collaborator' whose knowledge of the desert was 'crucial to the German side and could have meant a different history for all of us'.

In all this, Ondaatje publicly expressed his satisfaction that the film, as directed and scripted by Anthony Minghella, was faithful to his novel. And in a letter to the press he stressed the point that it was not a documentary or a history lesson 'but an interpretation of human emotions – love, desire, betrayals in war and betrayals in peace – in a historical time'.

It holds no sympathy for Nazis . . . It is about forgiveness, how people come out of a war . . . If a novelist or dramatist or film-maker is to be censored or factually tested every time he or she writes from historical event, then this will result in the most uninspired works . . .

Quite apart from the fact that in the film the time-scale in which the fictional Almasy's dilemma is enacted is completely out of kilter, Professor Hurka's moral question itself is a non-starter so far as the real-life Almasy is concerned. He was not guilty of betraying a cause in which he should have believed: the defeat of Nazism. He was, after all, a reserve officer in the Hungarian Air Force and Hungary was an ally of Nazi Germany, so that it is surely stretching an otherwise legitimate point to characterize his conduct as 'betrayal'. It was either opportunistic, in that he saw working for the Nazi war effort as a chance to return to the desert he loved, or else ideological, in that he truly believed in Hitler's war aims. Which of these was his motivation is the question at the heart of this biography.

While it is true that in many essential respects – not the least the matter of sexual preference – the fictional Almasy and the 'real' Almasy are very different men, they are very much alike in one thing: they are equally enigmatic, equally elusive. Whenever the researching biographer imagines he has pinned the man's character down, some perplexing new fact emerges to raise new uncertainties and – to mix the metaphor – the focus blurs again.

Was he, as the British suspected, a pre-war spy for the Italians or, as the Italians suspected, a pre-war spy for the British? Perhaps he was both; perhaps he was neither.

Was he a genuine Nazi sympathizer or no more than a romantic royalist and traditionalist? Perhaps it was his insatiable love of the desert which swept all other considerations aside. Did he become a double agent serving British intelligence towards the end of the war and during the Cold War that followed? And if so, did he do so out of conviction or self-preservation? And if not a British intelligence 'asset' why else would MI6 have gone to considerable expense and trouble to help him escape from Hungary and return to Egypt? Crucially, by what means was he able in 1946 to beat a war crimes charge levelled against him by a Hungarian communist People's Court which might anyway have been expected to jail or even execute him simply for the crime of being 'a class enemy'?

It must be said that although Almasy was undoubtedly resourceful and brave – indeed, some of his fellow desert explorers thought him positively reckless – with a genuine love and profound knowledge of the desert and its inhabitants, there was also something rather louche about him. For many aspects of his life there is no surviving documentation. This is in part because his post-war private papers mysteriously vanished from his Cairo apartment after his death; in part because many of his pre-war papers are now inaccessible; in part because, as most homosexuals were forced to be in his day, he was secretive and something of a loner; and in part because any evidence of his connections with British intelligence remains locked in the secret archives of MI6.

All that said, Almasy remains a fascinating and little-recognized figure, the record of whose desert discoveries is a tribute to his dedication, determination, courage and skill.

As for the questions about his true motives, the answers will perhaps have to be found – by the reader as much as the author – in 'the balance of probabilities', a doctrine to which historians and biographers so often have to take recourse.

Chapter 1

Laszlo Ede Almasy was born on 22 August 1895 into a dysfunctional and disgruntled family – dysfunctional because his parents were disastrously mismatched; disgruntled because, despite their ancient lineage, the Almasys lacked a noble title.

Laszlo's birthplace, Castle Borostyanko in western Hungary (and since 1920 Burg Bernstein in eastern Austria), was the recently purchased property of his paternal grandfather, Eduard Almasy. Having sold off a valuable but less prestigious estate, Eduard had bought the castle in the hope that so fine a property would enhance his hopes of achieving the aristocratic status that he felt, not without reason, was his family's due.

Castle Borostyanko had a venerable history. It was the loftiest of a string of fortresses peppering the Austrian–Hungarian borderland, where a German-speaking majority of peasants and townsfolk lived under the generally benign tutelage of a Hungarian-speaking Magyar elite. Down the ages the Burgenland (Land of Castles), as the region was named after it was ceded to Austria under the post-World War I Treaty of Trianon, had been fought over by the Austrians, the Hungarians, the Turks and others more exotic, such as the Dukes of Anjou. From the thirteenth century the castle had been the stronghold of a succession

of Austrian and Hungarian robber barons. Struck by light-
ning in 1617 and partially destroyed by the consequent
explosion of its powder magazine, it had been rebuilt in the
Baroque style before passing into the hands of the Counts
of Battyanhy in the mid seventeenth century. They held
it until 1864 when – unlikely as it may sound – it became
the property of an Irishman named Edward Egan, estate
manager of Count Gustav, last of the Battyanhys. Twenty-
eight years after that Egan's heirs sold the castle and
demesnes to Eduard Almasy.

The Hapsburgs' Austro-Hungarian Empire was then at
its zenith and the village of Borostyanko, nestling in the
shadow of the Almasys' newly acquired country seat, presented a façade of well-ordered rural prosperity. It was an
idyllic spot – a conglomeration of some fifty yellow-, green-
and pink-washed cottages, each adorned with decorated
casements and doorways ample enough to allow horse-
drawn carts into their enclosed farmyards. In the village
centre was a pond fringed by ancient chestnut trees and
noisily populated by ducks and geese. There was also a fine
fifteenth-century church and an architecturally outstanding
eighteenth-century Baroque hostelry, the Hotel Post.

Nowadays, in the aftermath of two world wars, one cold
war and two dictatorial regimes, Nazi and communist,
the idyll is scarcely a memory. Though still surrounded
by farmland and some distance from any major town,
Bernstein-that-was-Borostyanko has more the ambience of
a sanitized suburb than a rural hamlet. The old farmhouses
have gone, the duckpond has been drained and the Hotel
Post has been replaced by a modern café. Only the castle,

albeit now a hotel, remains largely unchanged: it still contains a dungeon complete with rack and whipping bench, an armoury and an 'alchemist's kitchen'.

Its massive buttressed walls enclose a flagstoned courtyard and under the portcullis entrance the main staircase is decorated with the escutcheons of its previous owners. A corridor encircles the ground floor, containing a *Rittersaal*, or knights' hall, where the Magyar knights of old used to gather under a magnificent stuccoed ceiling featuring scenes from Greek mythology. On the first and subsequent floors are the bedrooms, in one of which Laszlo Almasy was born. The proprietors of the present-day hotel, Laszlo's niece and her husband, like to boast that those bedrooms contain no modern conveniences. Rather, they are crammed with antiques and heated in cold weather by wood fires, while the bathrooms, though necessarily not of medieval origin, are proudly and ponderously old-fashioned.

Ownership of a castle and estate so steeped in history undoubtedly conferred prestige on the untitled Eduard Almasy, although one would need to delve deep into the mysteries of Hungarian genealogy and the intricacies of Austro-Hungarian political culture to understand exactly *why* he lacked a title. One explanation offered by a respected genealogical source is that the Almasys were originally counts, but were reduced to the ranks when they sided with the revolutionaries of 1848 against the alien Hapsburgs.* A rival school of genealogy, however, holds that in the days

---

* In 1866, following Austria's defeat in war against Prussia, the Hapsburgs gave in sufficiently to Magyar pressure to reconstitute their realm as a dual kingdom comprising Austria and a semi-autonomous Hungary.

of Hapsburg rule it was constitutionally impossible for a Hungarian aristocratic title to be revoked.

Whatever the truth of that arcane controversy, it was apparently not entirely unknown for a Magyar family at the end of the nineteenth century to boast noble descent but no title; in terms understandable to the present-day British the Almasys may best be thought of as landed gentry with above-average wealth and social connections.

Despite his celebrated accomplishments as a zoologist, ethnographer and explorer, Eduard Almasy's only son Gyorgy was a disappointment to his father: he had made a marriage that did nothing at all to forward the old man's dynastic ambitions. And having made so unsuitable a match, Gyorgy seemed to be doing everything possible to ensure that his marriage failed.

The bride he brought home from a visit to Verona – an Austro-Hungarian possession until a united Italy achieved independence in 1861 – was Ilona Pittoni, a spirited young woman who claimed direct descent from Giambattista Pittoni (1687–1767), a Venetian painter of great distinction and international acclaim.* But Eduard was not impressed by her artistic antecedents: she was not of Magyar blood, her family had not prospered in recent years and she herself had been reduced to singing in the chorus at the Arena, Verona's celebrated opera house, an occupation which in those days was considered to be more colourful than respectable.

* His paintings – mainly of religious or classical subjects – are exhibited in the world's greatest art galleries, including the Louvre, the Hermitage, the Getty and the National Gallery.

In 1890 Ilona presented Gyorgy with their first child, a boy named Janos. In 1893, after Eduard had purchased Castle Borostyanko and the young couple had moved in with him, came a daughter, Gyorgina, and two years after that Laszlo was born. By this time the marriage was in serious difficulty. Gyorgy's twin passions were the cause of the problem – his quest for the roots of the Magyar people, deep in the mountains and plains of Central Asia, and his no less eager search for extra-marital adventures in the salons and boudoirs of Central Europe.

For all his family's current fealty to Hungary's Austrian overlords, Gyorgy Almasy was a deep-dyed Magyar nationalist. He was obsessed about discovering the origins of his ethnic forebears who, as legend had it, had ridden out of the steppes of Kirghizia and Kazakhstan and the mountains of Tien-Shan during the Dark Ages to conquer and populate the Hungarian Plain.

Not for Gyorgy the mundane demands of home and family or the responsibilities of estate management; one 'scientific' expedition was followed in short order by another, and the search for primal roots punctuated by the search for private pleasures – in particular in the arms of a favourite mistress in San Marino, another of Austria-Hungary's former possessions in northern Italy.

His infidelities abroad and lack of affection at home soon became more than Ilona was willing to endure. She was by no means typical of the meek and submissive women of her time and social class. What was more, her once disapproving father-in-law was beginning to take her side. As for the three children, although shielded behind a screen of nannies and governesses, they were growing up in an atmosphere of persistent parental bickering.

As the rows became increasingly shrill, grandfather Eduard was fast losing patience with his wandering son's extravagances, which were wearing an ever-enlarging hole in the estate's revenues from rents and the quarrying of its unique deposits of semi-precious serpentine stone.*

Lasci, as Laszlo was now called by family and friends, seems to have been particularly affected by the unhappy household atmosphere. Enthralled on the one hand by his father's tales of exploration and adventure in remote places, he was distressed on the other by his mother's wretchedness and the growing rift between his parents. This may account for his inability in later life to make and sustain lasting relationships.

It may also account for his educational backwardness. While his older brother Janos was being schooled at the Gymnasium in Graz, the nearest major city, Lasci was being tutored at home by Dominican friars from the nearby Koszeg Gymnasium. They instructed him in various subjects from the age of nine, but were invariably disappointed by the results: although by no means stupid, he failed in mathematics, Latin and geometry and his marks in other subjects were no better than poor.

After four years the Dominicans gave up on him and though he was subsequently sent to join Janos at the Graz Gymnasium he failed to make the grade there, too, for he

* The Borostyanko/Bernstein Castle estate was said to contain the world's only deposit of this green, jade-like stone, which is odd since *Bernstein* in German means amber, not jade.

had no interest in academic subjects. What *did* interest him was modern technology – automobiles and flying machines.

Aged only fourteen, he built himself a primitive glider – an extraordinarily bold achievement by one so young in the very infancy of heavier-than-air aviation. Launching the glider from a hilltop near the family *Schloss*, he managed to remain airborne for several seconds before crashing, Icarus-like, to earth, breaking a number of ribs. He spent the next several weeks in hospital.

While Lasci's ribs mended and his father was away on another expedition, his grandfather – at a loss what to do next about the boy's intermittent and so far unsatisfactory academic progress – hit on the idea of sending him to school in England. The old man may have hoped that if Lasci did not distinguish himself as a scholar he might at least learn the ways of the world's most admired imperial elite and become the simulacrum of an 'English gentleman'.

But if Eduard had ideas of Eton or Harrow for the educationally challenged Lasci he was to be disappointed. The boy was quite incapable of passing the most routine public school entrance examination, so, as a very distant second best, he was sent at fifteen to Berrow School, a crammer situated in a private house at 17 Carew Road, Eastbourne, under the tutelage of Mr Daniel W. Wheeler, MA, FRGS. There, Laszlo paid little more attention than before to his lessons but, still fired with enthusiasm for aviation, he joined the pioneering Eastbourne Flying Club, flew solo after only a few hours' training and won his first amateur pilot's licence at the age of seventeen – another remarkable achievement to match his semi-successful attempt to build a glider three years earlier.

As for his other great interest, the automobile, his driving licence records that in November 1913 he was fined one pound twelve shillings with eighteen shillings costs for 'driving a motor car at a dangerous speed' in Eastbourne. With that comparatively trivial event, Laszlo's future as a motorist and aviator was set.

Yet there was one direction, apart from his facility with modern machinery, in which the young Laszlo excelled: he had a formidable gift for languages. Effortlessly mastering spoken and written English, he was rapidly able to add it to his native Hungarian and German, the Italian he had learned at his mother's knee and the French he had picked up somewhere along the way.* He even had more than a smattering of conversational Russian, learned from a Kirghiz minstrel whom his father had brought home from one of his expeditions to Central Asia.

To round off his education for life, Laszlo had by now acquired an insatiable need for nicotine – even smoking his cassocked tutors' discarded cigarette stubs while being taught at home – and from adolescence on he was seldom to be seen without a cigarette in his hand or mouth.

While in England, he also joined the Boy Scout movement, founded in 1908 by the British Boer War hero, Sir Robert Baden-Powell. He remained a keen and promi-

---

* He was later to add Arabic to his repertoire, bringing to an impressive six the number of languages in which he was completely at home.

nent member of the Hungarian scouting movement into maturity and would personally escort Baden-Powell himself during an official visit to Hungary in 1933.

Shortly after Laszlo began his schooling in England, his grandfather finally lost patience with Gyorgy's extravagances, his failure to attend to the business of the estate and his neglect of his wife and children. In the old man's eyes, a few learned articles published in the proceedings of the Royal Hungarian Geographical Society did not compensate for those failings. Riding down to Szombatheley, the Vas County seat, Eduard went to his lawyer's office and drew up a will disinheriting Gyorgy and bequeathing his castle, lands and chattels on his death to his favourite and first-born grandson, Janos. He provided for Ilona and the two younger children by leaving them modest but adequate allowances. For the roving Gyorgy there was nothing but the right, when he deigned to be at home, to occupy a strictly delimited part of the castle.

After the will came the formal dissolution of the marriage. Civil divorce had been made lawful in Austria-Hungary in the year of Laszlo's birth and although most of the Magyar upper classes, including the Almasys, were Roman Catholics, they were by no means universally averse to this unusually liberal (for the time) dispensation. Accordingly, the marriage of Gyorgy and Ilona was dissolved by mutual agreement in August 1912.

It may have been deliberate policy on Eduard's part to bring all this about during the absence in Eastbourne of Laszlo, the most sensitive of his three grandchildren. In mid June of 1914, Laszlo – by now tall, spare and elegant, with post-adolescent good looks that were somewhat impaired by a beaky, oversized nose – was finishing a final term at his Eastbourne crammer when a Serbian student named Gavrilo Princip fired 'the shots that were heard around the world'. His two bullets killed Archduke Franz Ferdinand, heir to the Austro-Hungarian Empire, and his wife, Sophie, Duchess of Hohenberg, as they drove in an open car through Sarajevo, Bosnia's principal city. And although there was no evidence of Serbian government complicity in the crime, a vengeful Austro-Hungarian government saw it, in the words of its army chief of staff Conrad von Hotzendorf, as 'a godsend, or rather a gift from Mars'.

As war loomed Laszlo hurried home in great excitement and, with brother Janos, joined the fashionable 11th Regiment of Hussars. The crisis deepened and the European powers, inescapably entangled in two hostile alliances, drifted in what Winston Churchill would call 'a dull cataleptic trance' towards universal conflict. Happily for Laszlo's peace of mind – given his recently acquired regard for the British – his country's war aims were directed eastward, against Serbia and its mighty ally, tsarist Russia.

When the shooting began in August 1914 Laszlo became involved, first against the Serbs, in an offensive across the River Drina, and later against the invading Russians in Carpathia, where he was decorated for gallantry in action. In mid 1916 both he and Janos found themselves at home on leave where they posed for a studio photograph with their proud father, himself in uniform as a headquarters staff officer. They make a handsome trio, exuding the style and elegance of the Austro-Hungarian Empire's final years, but concealing the underlying tensions between the two brothers – one to come into a fortune, the other to inherit a pittance – and the father who had neglected them and ill-treated their mother.

Instead of returning to the Russian front when his leave ended, Laszlo was transferred to the fledgling Austro-Hungarian Air Force where he would be of greater use to the war effort. As an aviator rather than a light cavalryman, he now found himself engaged against the Italians who had belatedly joined the Allies against the Central Powers in 1915.

The war was going well for the Hapsburg Empire. By mid 1916 Austria-Hungary was master of the Balkans and had driven the Russians from its soil. But the cost in lives was frightful and even among the originally ardent supporters of war there was growing disillusion. In Budapest, a young poet summed it up: '*We wanted something good, beautiful, brave / But came disaster, sorrow, anguish.*' In March 1918, during a futile Austro-Hungarian offensive in northern Italy, Almasy was in action over the Alps when his aircraft was badly shot up by an Italian fighter. Wounded, he was barely able to limp back over the foothills to crash-land in a field. Mended and released from hospital, he was not sent back into action, but spent the last few months of the Great War as a flight instructor at air force headquarters in Wienerneustadt.

By now – and even though Russia had surrendered to Germany and descended into revolution – the Austro-Hungarian war effort was faltering. The venerable emperor Franz Josef had been succeeded by the less than charismatic

Karl IV and the dual kingdom was beginning to fall apart. The end came in late October 1918, when Vienna sued for peace. In the following year, under the Treaties of St Germain and Trianon, Austria was separated from its twin, Hungary, and reduced to a relatively insignificant state of eight million.

Hungary itself – helpless and now under a revolutionary regime headed by the communist Bela Kun – was dismembered, losing chunks of territory to its neighbours, Romania and Bulgaria and, ironically, also to rump Austria which was given Almasy's mainly German-speaking home province.

In the turbulent early post-war years, Almasy again took up arms. This time it was to join the counter-revolutionary and nationalist forces who overthrew the Bela Kun regime in 1919, massacring thousands of pro-communists in Budapest, and going on to repel an invasion by the Romanians.

These anti-communist nationalist forces were led by Admiral Miklos Horthy, formerly commander of the Austro-Hungarian navy,* who set himself up as Regent – and in effect the ultimate dictator – of Hungary. The nationalists were by no means all keen on this arrangement. Some of the most traditional, Almasy included, did not want some jumped-up regent: they wanted a king and a Hapsburg king at that. Accordingly, they remained misguidedly loyal to Karl IV, the last of the Hapsburg monarchs, by then in exile in Switzerland.

* Landlocked Austria-Hungary had an outlet to the Mediterranean through its possessions in Trieste and along the Croatian littoral and also maintained a handful of small craft on the Danube.

At Easter 1921 Karl returned clandestinely to Hungary in a bid to reclaim at least the Hungarian half of the defunct dual kingdom. His melodramatic arrival on the scene during a dinner given by the Roman Catholic Bishop of Szombatheley for a visiting Egyptian princeling has been described by the bishop's niece, the New York society hostess Mrs Hannah Van Horne. The Almasy brothers were present at table, Laszlo having organized a hunting party for the Egyptian prince from the bishop's summer residence.

Lasci and Janos were friends of my family [writes Mrs Van Horne] and interesting, mysterious and intelligent . . . Lack of title was a sore point with them . . . The Bishop of Szombatheley at that time was Count Janos Mikes, my father's younger brother. My sister was Princess Karl Auersperg. She was staying with our uncle in Szombatheley at the time . . . They, with other guests and priests, were sitting at the dinner table when the butler asked the bishop to follow him downstairs, as a guest had arrived who wished to speak to him. Then Lasci Almasy came to the table and, after whispering something in his ear, asked the bishop to go downstairs. My uncle then got up and followed Lasci. He saw a man sitting in an open car, disguised by the automobilist's driving helmet and dark glasses or goggles. He got a shock when this person took the goggles off. He recognized this man as his king.

King Karl set up temporary headquarters in the palace of the bishop, where royalist officers rallied to his side. Almasy was appointed the royalists' transport officer and was given the honour of driving King Karl to Budapest.

There, in what had formerly been his own palace, Karl confronted Horthy who assured him that he was willing to help him reclaim the throne but secretly conspired to have him forced back into exile. The majority of the Hungarian officer corps had by now thrown in their lot with Horthy and faced with this situation – not to mention the open hostility of the victorious British and French governments to any Hapsburg restoration – the Pretender felt obliged to return empty-handed to Switzerland.

This was not the end of Karl's attempts to recover the throne, or of Almasy's attempts to help him do so. In October of the same year the Pretender was flown back to western Hungary, landing on the estate of a sympathetic landowner. This time he proceeded to Budapest in an armoured train, again with an escort of royalist officers including the ever-faithful Almasy.

This second attempt had elements of farce as well as melodrama. The train moved so slowly – stopping at almost every station en route so that Karl could receive the acclaim of his subjects and pick up a few more royalist troops – that Horthy had plenty of time to organize an effective opposition. When the train reached the outskirts of the capital it was met by an improvised force of pro-Horthy university students and 1914–18 war veterans.

In the brief and relatively bloodless clash that followed, the main casualty was Karl's credibility. His force was defeated, his train was turned back and he was sent away again,* but not before he rewarded some of his most zealous

---

* He ended up in Madeira, where he died in April the following year.

supporters, among them the young Almasy, by conferring titles on them.

Thus Laszlo became a count, though perhaps it would be more correct to call him a quasi-count, for the title was never confirmed by the Hungarian parliament and, although he would be known as 'Count Almasy' in Egypt, he was never able to use the title at home.

During the next few years the not quite count was employed by Bishop Mikes as his secretary and huntsman. There is a degree of mystery about their relationship. In later life Laszlo would claim that the wealthy nobleman–cleric was his uncle and that he expected to inherit at least part of his fortune. This may have been a ploy to fend off Laszlo's many creditors. In fact, there seems to have been no blood link between them, one account holding that the two met during the war on the Eastern Front where Mikes was an army chaplain. Whatever the truth of that, Bishop Mikes made no provision for Laszlo in his will.*

While eking out a patronage living in the service of his 'uncle', Laszlo took a course in motor mechanics and, more befitting a Magyar country gentleman, passed his days hunting boar, bear and wildfowl in the dense forests around Bernstein. In more up-to-date vein, he also became a motor rally star, driving for the Steyr Automobile Works, head-quartered in the nearby city of Graz. Both activities were

---

*Mikes was killed in the spring of 1945 by an American bomber (which dropped its load on Szombatheley Cathedral and the adjoining episcopal palace, apparently mistaking it for a factory complex), and not, as published elsewhere, while trying to save a local girl from being raped by Russian soldiers.

to stand him in good stead in the future: he made valuable contacts among prominent sprigs of the idle-rich Egyptian royalty and aristocracy who maintained hunting lodges nearby and joined his forays into the forest, while at the same time honing his skills while rally driving for his future motorized explorations of the desert.

Most importantly, his performance as a driver–mechanic brought him an offer from Steyr that he could not refuse. Having diversified from their core activity as makers of small-arms, Steyr were now determined to make a global mark as motor manufacturers and invited Laszlo to go to Cairo as their representative, with a brief to establish their brand name throughout the Middle East and Africa. Driven to earn a living and setting aside the Magyar gentry's traditional disdain for trade or commerce – even for the professions – Laszlo gladly accepted the offer.

Chapter 2

In the same year that Laszlo went to Egypt his grandfather died, his father moved his personal quarters to a remoter part of Burg Bernstein and his brother Janos came into his inheritance.

Suave, handsome and with more conventional charm than Laszlo, Janos now found his new status as a major landowner beginning to conflict with his bachelor life as country gentleman in Bernstein and urban boulevardier in Budapest. He had become a 'catch' and, as master of Burg Bernstein, had aroused the interest of the lordly Esterhazy family.

Before the 1914–18 war the Esterhazys had been Hungary's biggest landowners and, so it was said, privately richer than even the imperial Hapsburgs. For generations, they had also been great patrons of the arts. At their palace in Eisenstadt, not far from Borostyanko/Bernstein, they had employed Joseph Haydn (1732–1809) – the most celebrated composer of his day – as their court musician and *Kappelmeister*. Even amid the chaos and social disruption of post-war life they remained at the pinnacle of wealth, taste and social standing throughout Central Europe.

But they had a domestic problem: one of their daughters, Princess Maria Rosa, had been thrown by her horse at the age of sixteen and crippled for life. Confined to a wheelchair, she would never be able to bear children and consequently, for all her beauty and blue blood, her chances of marrying into a family of equal social standing were nil.

For his part, Janos Almasy had acceptable ancestry, a fine castle and extensive land but little money and no title. The social cachet that would go with marriage to an Esterhazy was as appealing to him as the opportunity to marry off an otherwise unmarriageable and ageing daughter was to her parents. So in 1929, by which time she was the same age as the century, the pale and pious Princess Maria wed Janos Almasy in the Esterhazys' ornate chapel at Eisenstadt.

The festivities over, the newly-weds returned to Burg Bernstein where thenceforth the devout princess was to be stranded in her wheelchair in a ground-floor suite – a tragically beautiful and almost ethereal presence to rival the building's more conventional ghost, the so-called White Lady, who was said to flit about the corridors at night.

Princess Maria's immobility and the wealth she had brought with her gave Janos ample opportunity to resume and expand his dual life as rural squire and man about town. Now he was a frequent visitor to the fleshpots not only of Budapest but also of Vienna, Berlin, Paris and Cairo* where, as an acquaintance would later say, he was always to be seen 'surrounded by beautiful women',† attracted as much by his saturnine good looks and easy charm as by his free-spending habits.

By contrast, the lean, hawk-nosed Laszlo was to remain

* Then a far more Europeanized city than nowadays.
† Nor was he averse, when at home, to exercising his *droit de seigneur* over the local peasant girls.

a lifelong bachelor, perennially hard up in a well–off kind of way, and certainly not without charm, but with no interest at all in the opposite sex. Childhood memories of his parents' scalding rows and the trauma of their divorce may have been a factor in his inability to relate to women and his evolving homosexual inclinations.

Some believe that he may also have been influenced by the homoerotic subtext of the cabbalistic and necromantic mumbo-jumbo that seemed to fascinate the other male members of his family.* But this seems unlikely: Laszlo was an altogether practical man, far more likely to be found with a spanner in his hand than a crackpot notion in his head.

In the winter of 1926, at the wheel of a sturdy Steyr touring model and accompanied by his fellow Burgenlander and future brother–in–law, Prince Antal Esterhazy, Almasy began his African career by making a pioneering test drive from Cairo to Aswan, six hundred miles alongside the Nile on an unmade and often imperceptible desert track. From there they drove across the forbidding gravel flats of the Nubian Desert to Khartoum, capital of Anglo–Egyptian Sudan, where the White Nile and the Blue Nile converge.

From Khartoum, Almasy and Esterhazy followed the Blue Nile and then its tributary, the Dinder, until they reached a game-rich area (now a national park) where they took full advantage of the plentiful opportunities for

---

* Books in the locked cabinets of Bernstein Castle to this day include such arcana as Vehlow's *Astrologie*, Eliphas Levi's *Salomonische Schlussel*, Papus's *Traité élémentaire de science occulte* and *The Tarot of Bohemia*. The cabinets also contain an array of pentacles and related black magic paraphernalia.

shooting and fishing. Almasy has left us no description of this primeval terrain but he must have found it little changed from when the British explorer Samuel Baker had reached it some sixty years before.

Baker had noted that the region 'was uninhabited except by wandering Arabs and their flocks that migrate at the commencement of the rainy season, when this land becomes a mere swamp and swarms with seroti fly'.

The average breadth [of the river] is about 110 yards; the banks are about 50 feet high and the immediate vicinity is covered with thick jungle . . . The Arabs assured me that the crocodile in this river were more dangerous than in any other . . . I found a herd of hippopotamus, of which I shot two . . .

For Almasy, in a motor vehicle, the journey was ground-breaking, giving him the opportunity to sharpen his skills at motor maintenance under difficult conditions and to learn the art of navigating over uncharted terrain.

In the following year Steyr sent several vehicles, including some experimental models, to Cairo for an international automobile exhibition. From his headquarters at the Mena House Hotel, near the Great Pyramids of Giza on the outskirts of Cairo, Almasy and a French-Canadian driver named Leblanc 'tortured' their six-wheeled experimental cars – advanced for the day, but archaically cumbersome and deceptively tinny-looking by today's standards – with 'indescribable tests' in the desert.

It was here that Almasy learned the knack of tackling sand dunes by driving full tilt at the 'easy' windward side, sailing up to the top, then turning sharply sideways at the summit to slide broadside-on down the steeper leeward side. Although a nerve-wracking experience for the uninitiated, this was not as perilous a manoeuvre as it might seem. Sensing its commercial possibilities, Almasy and Leblanc staged a number of 'thrill rides' for adventurous, well-to-do tourists until the practice was banned by the Egyptian authorities on safety grounds.

Emboldened by what he had learned of desert driving so far, Almasy next embarked on a journey that, if his account is to be fully believed, might have ended his career prematurely. This was a 220-mile (350-km.) drive from the Pyramids to the remote and isolated Bahariya Oasis, set amid the infamous Abu Moharig dune barrier that stretches from the Qattara Depression, about 50 miles from the Mediterranean coast, to the Kharga Oasis, 560 miles to the south. Recklessly, Almasy undertook this journey in one car, entirely without back-up in case of breakdown, and by his own account with no reserves of food and only one 10-litre can of water. He had a Bedouin guide but no maps, the car was underpowered and heavy for its size and, as he would later claim, the inhabitants of the oasis were astonished when this, to them, extraordinary machine and its unlikely driver appeared out of the dunes.

Though isolated and impoverished, the Bahariya Oasis had been continuously inhabited since Classical times. There were a number of Roman ruins within its 25 by 15 miles boundary and it contained archaeological evidence of a considerable Christian community until the sixteenth century AD, when expansionist Islam finally supplanted the prevailing Coptic culture of the oasis-dwellers.

If Almasy noticed the evidence of a historic past he failed to mention it in his account of the trip. He did, however, record that the inhabitants of Bahariya killed a goat for a feast in his honour before seeing him off with blessings on the return trip to Cairo. This time he was well stocked with food and water for the journey and, in retrospect, he was to share the general astonishment that he had conquered the dunes and reached his destination so ill-prepared.

Notwithstanding Almasy's pioneering achievement, it should be recorded that there did exist a rough camel track from the outskirts of Cairo to the oasis* and that, although arrival by car may have been unprecedented in 1927, camel caravans taking dates from the palm groves of Bahariya to the markets of Cairo travelled regularly between the two points.

In 1929, following a return visit to Sudan the previous year, in which he led a group of titled Hungarian big-game hunters, Almasy embarked on a major experimental trip through Kenya, Uganda and Sudan to Egypt. He was accompanied this time by his wealthy friend and client, Prince Ferdinand of Lichtenstein, and Rudi Mayer, an Austrian cameraman they had engaged to make a film record of the safari.

Starting in a snowstorm from a wintry Vienna in two sturdy Steyr XX pick-up trucks, and thence to Marseilles for a sea voyage through the Mediterranean and the Suez

---

*Now supplanted by a tarmac highway, with a parallel main-line rail track to serve a population of thirty thousand.

Canal, Almasy's party disembarked at Mombasa on the
East African coast. From there they made their way through
Kenya and Tanganyika, hunting and filming as they
went, with Almasy, wherever he could find a telegraph
office, cabling technical reports back to the Steyr factory in
Austria.

Mayer recorded their every move on his hand-cranked
camera, but unaccountably his silent film was never to be
shown in public until, seven decades later and long after his
death, his son Kurt found the negative reels in a drawer in
his attic in Vienna. By that time Ondaatje's novel and the
subsequent Hollywood film had brought Almasy's name to
world attention and Kurt Mayer turned his father's forgotten reels into an award-winning documentary for television. It gives a vivid impression of the safari – and of the
young Almasy at the cusp of his adventurous career. It was
an 'unforgettable expedition', he would write.

Just a couple of days out of Mombasa we see Almasy
repairing a washed-away bridge over the Tsavo river in
southern Kenya, then guiding the two Steyr trucks over the
torrent across the rickety boards he had just laid down.
Only from his written account of the trip do we learn
that Almasy performed this demanding feat of impromptu
bridge-building while suffering from a fever of 102°F
(39°C). Further on, he demonstrates his hands-on skill
as a motor mechanic by replacing a rear spring, broken in
their passage over rock-strewn terrain. While in camp on
the Masai game plains, Almasy's morning ablutions are
rudely interrupted by a large scorpion, scuttling across the
table towards him while he shaves. We see him snare the

venomous intruder by slipping a wire noose over its tail and lifting it from the table.

Some of the filmed incidents might seem distasteful to today's more politically and socially sensitive post-colonial generation. We see Almasy and Lichtenstein paying young native girls to dance for them – some pre-pubertal, others a little older, jiggling their naked, immature breasts and buttocks for the amusement of the two white *bwanas*. After the dance display Almasy gives the girls cigarettes and teaches them how to smoke. 'Don't blow into it, draw on it' reads the film caption. In other sequences, we see Almasy and Lichtenstein blazing away at a variety of game animals – gazelle, zebra, wildebeest, elephant and water buffalo – some for meat, some for trophies and others, it seems, for the sheer thrill of the kill. In one scene they drag the corpse of a zebra behind their vehicle as bait for a hyena.

They lay a vicious steel-leg trap beside the zebra's corpse, attach the trap with a cord to its leg, camouflage the trap with dead grass, and wait in hiding. When the hyena turns up the trap snaps shut on its right leg. It struggles frantically to get free and Almasy ends its agony with a shot. A film caption tells us that the hyena had 'caused grave injury to the herds of our hosts', the local tribespeople.

After driving through Uganda and into Sudan they make what Almasy would later claim to be the first-ever crossing by car of the notorious Sudd, an enormous swamp straddling the White Nile south of Khartoum. The Sudd covers 6,370 square miles (16,500 sq. km.) in the dry winter months and expands to twice that size during the rains of summer. And as Alan Moorehead, the celebrated historian of the Nile, has written, 'there is no more formidable obstacle in the world'.

The Nile loses itself in a vast sea of papyrus ferns and rotting vegetation, and in that foetid heat there is a spawning of tropical life that can hardly have altered very much since the beginning of the world . . . This region is neither land nor water. Year by year the current keeps bringing down more floating vegetation and packs it into solid chunks perhaps twenty feet thick and strong enough for an elephant to walk on. But then this debris breaks away in islands and forms again in another place.

Almasy and Lichtenstein arrived in the dry season and decided to attempt a crossing.

Picking their route carefully, they steer clear of places where they might become bogged down. Occasionally they leave their vehicles and proceed on foot, guided by local Dinka tribesmen, to visit villages that had never seen a white man before. At one of these they proceed by native boat, a hollowed-out tree trunk, to where they can observe a herd of knee-deep swamp elephants. Almasy shoots one of them, cutting off its tail to fashion into a good luck bracelet and removing its tusks as trophies for Lichtenstein's billiard room. In another sequence we see scores of Dinka, up to their chests in the swamp, spearing fish for food in a welter of foaming water and blood.

The high point of Rudi Mayer's film comes with a fortuitous invasion of Dinka territory by warriors of the neighbouring Nuer tribe. We see the Dinka perform a war dance as they prepare to do battle, but before the two tribes clash the colonial British intervene to prevent a bloodbath.

A Nile steamer brings a company of Sudan Defence Force infantrymen with their British officers, while a Royal Air Force seaplane lands on the river, bringing a senior officer from headquarters. The SDF set up camp and the men practise bayonet drill before going into action. There is no footage of the fighting – the colonial British were not going to let a cameraman get close to the action – but after the Nuer have been driven off we see several of them as prisoners, chained hand and foot.

The British tell Almasy and Lichtenstein that their way ahead is clear, but three hours down the track towards Sobat, a Nile steamer stopping point, they are surrounded by rifle-toting Nuer. 'A resolute and friendly manner relieves the critical situation' reads the caption accompanying a sequence in which Almasy, Lichtenstein and Mayer show the wondering Nuer their guns, binoculars and camera equipment. In his published version, Almasy gives a somewhat different flavour to their encounter with the Nuer, claiming that they escaped only after he had performed an intimidating feat of 'magic'.

This consisted of convincing them to stand hand in hand in a circle [while I] gave the end of one of the motor cables into the hand of one and sat the other end onto the bonnet. I shook them with the high voltage current until I was certain that we could escape before they were able to lift their sore arms for their weapons.

At Sobat, Almasy's party crossed the Nile on a native ferry, gingerly, one car at a time, the vehicles straddled precariously on grooved runners laid across the beam of the boat. Once across, they made their way past the Nuba Mountains towards the White Nile's twin, the Blue Nile, and Sennar, the site of a newly built hydroelectric dam. From there they motored downstream, skirting the west bank, to Khartoum where the two Niles join.

At Khartoum, Mayer left the party, his contract fulfilled, and after spending a couple of weeks in the Sudanese capital, Almasy and Lichtenstein drove on north through the forbidding Nubian Desert with three newly hired Sudanese servants, heading for Wadi Halfa on the Sudanese–Egyptian frontier. By reaching Wadi Halfa they had covered 7,500 miles of the world's toughest driving terrain since leaving Mombasa. They still had seven days of hard desert driving ahead of them before reaching Cairo, the end of the safari.

This last leg of the trip, brief earlier outings excepted, was Almasy's first major encounter with Egypt's Western Desert, or the Libyan Desert as it is called by geographers. Much as he had relished his East African safaris, this was an encounter that confirmed his burgeoning conviction that his destiny was to be found amid the dunes and the sand-and-gravel wastes of the eastern Sahara, rather than the game plains and forested hills of equatorial Africa.

That destiny was to be intimately bound up with modern technology in the shape of the aeroplane and in particular of the automobile, which was beginning to open up uncharted areas of the desert hitherto considered inaccessible, even to the wilderness-bred camel.

On both practical and aesthetic grounds, the more traditional of the small band of European desert explorers of that day would strenuously disapprove of the use of cars and trucks for this purpose. Typical and most articulate of these was Wilfred Thesiger, the redoubtable Englishman later famous for his pioneering camel-back exploration of the Arabian Peninsula's Empty Quarter.

To Thesiger, the mere idea of introducing a product of the industrial world into a natural wilderness was anathema; to impose the cacophony and smells of the internal combustion engine on the unspoiled solitudes of the desert was little short of blasphemy. 'The life of the Bedu ended the first time a car appeared in the country,' he once said. By contrast, Almasy found the 'most perfect expression of total freedom' in driving at full speed across the desert, 'where the metallic hum of the engine melts into the howl of the wind and the mysterious sigh of the sand dunes'.

He was well aware that his life might depend on the reliability of one small engine part or the proper functioning of an instrument and that other people might wonder what was to be gained by taking such risks to explore a waterless wasteland of sand and rock. But in the desert, Almasy believed, one could escape the tensions and temptations of modern living and find one's real self. There, body and soul were cleansed and man felt 'nearer to the Creator'. 'The desert is terrible and it is merciless,' he would write, 'but to the desert all who once have known it must return.'

Chapter 3

Although it is sometimes called the Western Desert, because it lies west of the Nile, the Libyan Desert, as it is more correctly designated (even though much of it is in Egypt), is in fact the eastern, and by far the least accessible, half of the Sahara. Separated from the western Sahara by the Tibesti Mountains and a string of lesser highlands, the Libyan Desert covers an area of more than 1.5 million square miles (3,885,000 sq. km.) – about the size of the entire Indian subcontinent – an immensity that makes the rest of the world's deserts seem mere sandpits by comparison.

A series of escarpments, some of them higher than 1,000 feet, run east to west, parallel to the Mediterranean, down the length of the desert. At the base of some of these scarps, centuries of wind pressure have excavated extensive hollows deep enough to reach the underground water table and form oases. Running roughly north to south are three great sand seas, row upon row of parallel dunes, some of them 500 feet (150 m.) high, seeming to march endlessly into a hazy eternity. As Bill Kennedy Shaw, a pioneer of motorized desert travel, has written: 'There is nothing like these sand seas anywhere else in the world.'

Take an area the size of Ireland and cover it with sand. Go on pouring sand on it till it is two, three or four hundred feet deep.

Then with a giant's rake score the sand into ridges and valleys running north north west and south south east with the ridges, at their highest, five hundred feet from trough to crest.

This is the hottest, driest region on earth. Daytime temperatures have been known to reach 150°F (65°C) in the summer months, while at night they can drop to below freezing. Apart from the Bedouin with their camels and goats, hardly any living creature can survive here save the scorpion, the dung beetle and the sand viper.

Even today, with the benefits of satellite global positioning equipment, airconditioned four-wheel-drive vehicles, accurate maps and reliable, long-range light aircraft, this vast, blistering wilderness of sand, gravel plains, mud pans, rocky plateaus and dune barriers presents a formidable challenge to the traveller. How much more so in Almasy's day, when the slab-sided Model A Ford and the spruce-and-fabric De Havilland Tiger Moth were state of the art, airconditioning for vehicles was unknown, there were no reliable maps, and navigation across a landscape that was often featureless – and even more often transformed by mirages into a treacherous kind of dreamscape – had to be done by sextant, compass and theodolite (impossible when sandstorms obscured the sun and stars) aided by dead reckoning.

To add to these difficulties were the sudden fierce desert winds, as if blowing out of the gates of hell during the day and straight from the Arctic at night. Often these winds would bring with them blinding, choking sandstorms, some lasting for days on end. Apart from clogging up every natural orifice, these had the curious effect of charging the human body with electricity so that whenever one touched one's car, for instance, one received a small but by no means inconsiderable shock.

And always, of course, there was the crushing, enervating heat. On a summer day at noon, says Kennedy Shaw, the Libyan Desert is 'as good an imitation of Hell as one can imagine'.

You don't merely feel hot, you don't merely feel tired, you feel as if every bit of energy had left you, as if your brain was thrusting its way to the top of your head and you want to lie in a stupor till the accursed sun has gone down.

But for the traveller intrepid, resourceful and durable enough to shoulder such hardships the Libyan Desert had compensations beyond calculation. Late in the evening, when the sands cool quickly and the dunes throw long shadows, the Sand Sea is 'one of the most lovely things in the world', Kennedy Shaw would recall. At such a moment 'the desert repays in the beauty of a few short hours a hundred days of choking heat, bitter wind, driving sandstorm, thirst and discomfort'.

One factor that made travel in the Libyan Desert especially difficult by comparison with the far more intensively travelled western Sahara was the long distances between oases and the paucity of marked tracks. Despite the gallant efforts of a handful of late nineteenth- and early twentieth-century explorers, these handicaps rendered much of the Libyan Desert *terra incognita*, a blank on the map comparable in its mystery with Antarctica or with the interior of sub-Saharan Africa as it had been a century before Almasy's time.

In the intense heat even the infinitely durable if slow-moving camel could not be expected to plod on indefinitely without water, thus restricting travellers to a very few traditional trade routes linking one oasis with another. At its best the camel can go fifteen days without water and, with a light load, make about eighteen miles a day, giving it a maximum range of about 270 miles between water sources.

Plying traditional routes, the camel was a tempting prize for roving bands of Bedouin raiders, so that any caravan needed a strong force of armed men to protect it. Thus, it was not until the advent of the motor car extended the range and enhanced the security of the desert traveller that it became possible to go, as it were, off piste and explore and map the immensity of this desert rather than merely to sniff around its edges.

One of the first outsiders to venture into these forbidding wastes by motor vehicle was the vastly wealthy Egyptian Prince Kemal el Din who drove into the deep desert, hundreds of waterless miles south of Cairo, at the head of a fleet of experimental half-tracked and six-wheeled vehicles, locating and mapping a number of significant geographical features. Most notable of these was an enormous rock plateau, with walls 1,000 feet (300-plus m.) high and equal in area to Switzerland, which in 1926 Kemal named the Gilf Kebir – the Great Wall.★

★ It is not only Westerners who tend to 'discover' places that are already well known to the indigenous people. The Gilf Kebir was occasionally traversed by the non-Arab Tibou tribesmen and its existence known to the nomadic Bedouin. But to Prince Kemal, as to the settled population of the Nile Valley as a whole, its very existence was a revelation.

By the time Almasy came on the scene, a handful of British Army officers, headed by Royal Signals major Ralph Bagnold and including civilians such as Kennedy Shaw, had been bitten by the desert bug and – to the consternation and occasional derision of their peers and superiors, who thought they must be mad – were spending their off-duty time undertaking similar expeditions. Not for the cash-strapped 'Baggers' and his companions the custom-built Citroën six-wheelers and half-tracks ordered up at great expense by Prince Kemal – and which, anyway, were not good at tackling sand dunes – but rather the workaday Model A Ford, which was to become the invariable mode of transport of the desert pioneers, including Almasy once his connection with Steyr had been broken.

The virtues of the Ford for desert travel were many. It was light enough to be pushed clear, with the help of steel channels inserted under the rear wheels, if bogged down in soft sand; its chassis was flexible enough not to crack when moving over rocky ground; its design was simple enough for the crews to fit replacement parts and effect repairs; its petrol and oil consumption were low for the weight carried; its 24-horsepower, four-cylinder engine packed sufficient power for the demands to be made on it; its ground clearance was good and spare parts were readily obtainable.

The use of steel channels to extricate a Ford from soft sand was effective enough, but excruciatingly slow and arduous. The channels were about 5 feet long and weighed some 35 pounds (15 kg.). When a vehicle bogged down the crew dug out the wheels and inserted the channels in front of the rear wheels. The driver would rev his engine to the limit then let in the clutch while his companions pushed; the rear wheels would climb on to the tracks and – if all went well – inch forward to the channel ends. Then the whole process would be repeated – time after time in the searing desert heat. 'At the end of an hour we had made 300 yards, and we had six more miles to make,' said Michael Mason, recalling a journey he made across the Sand Sea with Bill Kennedy Shaw and others.

To add to its other virtues, the Ford was easy to adapt for desert travel. The early motorized explorers often removed its bonnet, doors, hoods and front mudguards to save weight and added a couple of leaves to the rear springs. They also tended to add a light wooden framework to the body to increase the load capacity, making it possible for each vehicle to carry petrol, food, water and personal kit to a total of 1,500 to 2,000 pounds (700 to 900 kg.).

Despite the widely held notion that Bagnold and company were mapping the desert in anticipation of a future war, they had no idea that their journeys might produce information of military significance; they were repeatedly risking their lives in the desert 'for the fun of it'. Fun it may have been, but Bagnold – solidly self-educated in hydrology, geophysics, oceanography and geography* –

* And subsequently the author of *The Physics of Blown Sand*, a scholarly work that was to become a standard reference manual used by the Mars programme of the US National Aeronautical and Space Administration (NASA).

made some very serious contributions to desert driving lore which may seem commonplace enough nowadays but were highly innovative at the time.

He had worked out how to stop radiators boiling dry, thus conserving vital water, by leading the radiator overflow through a rubber tube and into an improvised tank half full of water bolted to the running board of the car. There the steam would condense and turn back into water before being sucked back into the radiator.

He had worked out how to avoid bogging down on soft sand by drastically reducing tyre pressures (reinflating when the terrain changed to *serir*, a hard-packed sand plain) and if he did blunder into a patch of soft sand how to get free by the use of steel channels and rope ladders at the front end.

He had calculated how to avoid the distorting effects of the surrounding steel on a car's magnetic compass by perfecting a sun compass – a device which allowed a driver to calculate his bearing by the position of a shadow cast by a vertical needle on to a graduated dial. It was Bagnold, too, who was one of the first to discover that the daunting 300-foot sand dunes could be surmounted if one had the nerve to drive at them full tilt. As he would describe his first attempt to do so:

I increased speed to forty miles an hour, feeling like a small boy on a horse about to take his first big fence . . . A huge glaring wall of yellow shot up high into the sky about a yard in front of us. The lorry tipped violently backwards – and we rose as in a lift, smoothly without vibration. We floated up on a yellow

45

cloud. All the accustomed car movements had ceased; only the speedometer told us we were still moving fast. It was incredible . . .

Bagnold also had some vital advice on self-preservation for future desert travellers: never travel with only one vehicle and in case of breakdown always remain with your car:

. . . An extraordinarily powerful impulse urges one to move, anywhere, in any direction, rather than stay still and think it out. This psychological effect of the true desert has been the cause of nearly every desert disaster of recent years. Always the lost one leaves his broken-down aeroplane or car and begins an unreasoning trudge, somewhere – it does not matter where. The vehicle is found by planes or trackers, but the solitary, half-demented walker is too small to spot.

All this desert lore was acquired in Bagnold's and his companions' own time and at their own expense. These expeditions, he would say, were mere 'jaunts', carried out solely for 'pleasure, interest and excitement'. There may have been suspicions, but there is no hard evidence, that Almasy's motives were less altruistic. However that may be, he would similarly acquire his desert expertise the hard way and by emulation and unremitting trial and error.

It was only some years later, when he and 'Bagnold's Boys' went to war – albeit on opposite sides – that this shared expertise would be put to incisive military purposes.

Chapter 4

Almost from the time of his arrival in Egypt, Almasy had been fascinated – a fascination that was to grow into an obsession – by two desert legends: that of Zerzura, the fabled 'oasis of the small birds', supposedly guarded by two *djinns* and inhabited by strange black men speaking an unknown tongue, and that of the lost army of Cambyses, the fifth-century BC Persian conqueror of Egypt.

According to legend, endorsed by the ancient Greek historian Herodotus, Cambyses sent a fifty-thousand-man force to march 350 miles (560 km.) across the desert from Dakhla to occupy the northern Siwa Oasis, site of the temple of the oracle Jupiter Ammon, only to have the entire army engulfed and buried en route by a huge sandstorm.

But before embarking on the search for Zerzura and for traces of Cambyses' lost legion Almasy set himself the task of rediscovering and travelling a section of the Libyan Desert's notorious Forty Days Road, or Darb el Arba'in. This ancient and easternmost of four camel caravan routes from the tropical south to the north brought slaves and other 'commodities' from black Africa to Egypt. It stretched 1,400 miles (2,250 km.) from El Fasher in Sudan's Darfur Province to Assiut in Egypt's Nile Valley and derived its name from the average number of days' march it took to complete.

In 1793, the first European to travel the entire length of the Darb el Arba'in, W. G. Browne, went with a five-hundred-camel caravan valued overall at £115,000 – about £50 million in today's currency. It included 'slaves, male and female; camels; ivory; horns of the rhinoceros; teeth of the hippopotamus; ostrich feathers; gum, pimento; tamarinds made into round cakes; peroquets in abundance and some monkey and guinea fowl; copper, white in small quantity'.

Along this highway of riches, suffering and despair – down the ages until the British outlawed the slave trade through Sudan at the end of the nineteenth century – untold thousands of black African slaves had staggered, tormented by thirst, shackled together in pairs by forked logs attached to the neck, and driven on by guards with rhinoceros-hide whips. Those who fell by the wayside left their bones to mark the way, together with the skeletons of their captors' camels, thousands of which also perished en route, however well adapted their species might be to desert hardships. One British explorer who travelled the Darb from Selima to Assiut not long after Almasy counted an average of two hundred camel skeletons for every mile of the route.

Those blacks who made it alive to the notorious slave market at Assiut – a mere one-fifth of those who started, according to contemporary records – were promptly put up for sale, alongside the rest of their captors' wares.

In the four decades between the time the British stopped the slave trade and Almasy set out to find the Forty Days Road it had become obscured by wind-blown sand and virtually forgotten, except as yet another desert legend recounted by a few grizzled old *kabirs* (guides) who had plied the trail in their youth.

Almasy planned to link up with the Darb at about the halfway point, Selima Oasis, close to the Sudanese–Egyptian frontier. A Nile steamer took him and his travelling companion, Prince Ferdinand of Lichtenstein, to the frontier port of Wadi Halfa, a nondescript little town on the east bank of the Nile where rail and river traffic converged. The town sported an administrative district office, docks and engineering workshops, but was long past its late Victorian glory days as Kitchener's headquarters for the recapture of Khartoum from the Mahdist rebels.* Here Almasy and Lichtenstein disembarked with their vehicles and, accompanied by a *kabir* named Mohammed, an *askari* (armed guard) and two Sudanese servants, they took a ferry to the opposite bank and drove in tandem towards Selima, about 160 miles (270 km.) due west. The journey was considered by the British officials at Wadi Halfa to be a hazardous undertaking and before Almasy's party were allowed to proceed Lichtenstein had to leave a substantial cash deposit with the district commissioner to defray the expense of an air-and-land search should they become bogged down or otherwise lost.

In the event, most of the route was across a *serir* and the going was relatively uneventful until, about thirty miles short of Selima, the engine of Almasy's car seized up. A hole in the Steyr's oil-filter screen had allowed sand, blown

---

* And nowadays half-submerged by Lake Nasser, created by the backing up of the Nile during construction of the Aswan High Dam in 1960–70.

by a fierce cross-wind, to penetrate into the camshaft. An impromptu inspection revealed that the engine would have to be removed and taken back to Wadi Halfa for repairs.

In the other, undamaged, car Almasy took Lichtenstein and the *askari* to Selima, leaving them there to await his return while he went back to the crippled vehicle to pick up Mohammed and the two Sudanese. There he removed the engine and drove back with it and the three others to their starting point.

At Wadi Halfa, Almasy managed to lay his hands on a carborundum disc with which he ground smooth the sand-damaged end of the camshaft. Then he drove 130 miles (208 km.) back through the night to where he had left the crippled car. But his travails were not over: while trying to install the repaired engine he discovered that some vital small parts had been left behind in Wadi Halfa by one of the Sudanese. There was nothing for it but to drive back once again to retrieve the missing parts. Severely pressed for time, Almasy made the journey by night – extremely difficult driving, since his headlights gave the ground surface a uniform colouring making it hard to distinguish soft sand from hard.

By the time he had made the second 260-mile round trip, successfully installed the engine and started back towards Selima Oasis, Almasy was exhausted, not least because the temperature at noon was registering 136°F (58°C) in the shade. It was 9 June and no time to be in the desert at all. But at least Almasy had once again had the chance to test his skill and resourcefulness at carrying out complicated repairs and doing so under atrocious conditions.

In more ways than one, Almasy found Selima Oasis a lovely sight – 'a wonder of nature', as he would say. It was uninhabited, crescent-shaped, about half a mile long and dotted with palm clusters. Its water was clear and sweet and there seemed to be no transition between the surrounding wilderness of rock and sand and Selima's bright green vegetation. 'It is a true island in a sea of desolation,' said Almasy. The explorer W. G. Browne had recorded that it 'affords the best water of any place on the route', but that 'although there be verdure enough to relieve the eye from the dry sterility of the surrounding furnace, it affords no vegetable fit for the support either of man or beast'.

Browne added the legend that 'it had of old been inhabited by a princess who, like the Amazons, drew the bow and wielded the battle-axe, with her own hand; that she was attended by a large number of followers, who spread terror all over Nubia, &c; and that her name was Selime'. This desert legend seems even less likely than most, given the subservient position of women in Arab society. As Michael Mason, a later traveller, has remarked: 'I still believe Selima to have been a hard-mouthed old harridan battening upon the hunger and thirst of caravaneers.'

Setting out from Selima with Lichtenstein to pick up the Forty Days Road, Almasy located it soon enough, despite the decades of blown sand which had covered over the original tracks. Grim piles of bleached bones marked the route as far as the eye could see and with these as guidelines there was no need for the compass. Some of the camel skeletons lay with their necks arched back towards the spine, others with their necks outstretched. Mohammed explained that those with arched-back necks had been slaughtered, in accordance with Muslim ritual, so that their thirsty keepers could obtain the water stored in their stomachs.

But for all his impressive repertoire of desert lore, Mohammed proved able to guide the party only as far as El Sheb, the next oasis on their route, where the water was murky and foul-tasting. Beyond that the way was, to Mohammed, *terra incognita*, and from there on it was up to Almasy to find the route, either by the skeleton markers or by compass.

The next water was at Kassaba, yet another uninhabited small oasis, about 85 miles (135 km.) distant. There they found the wellhead choked by sand and Almasy set the Sudanese to work to clear it. A few feet down they found the water clear and good-tasting. Noticing the trail of a desert fox leading to the wellhead, Almasy ordered his Sudanese to build some stone steps so that in future the foxes would have access to the water. But his good intentions were to backfire: the following year Bagnold reached Kassaba and found a drowned fox in the well.

About 18 miles (30 km.) short of Kassaba, Almasy had lost sight of the trail of skeletons and after his party filled their water containers he climbed a steep scarp hoping to spot the Darb through his binoculars. Before him lay a vast plateau and through his glasses he could see hundreds of parallel trails marked by what from a distance looked like patches of sprinkled white sugar. They were skeletons. He had found the Forty Days Road again and at this point it was so wide that he got out his tachometer to measure it. It was no less than 7 miles (12 km.) across.

From Kassaba their next water source at Bir el Murr was 60 miles (100 km.) away and not an oasis but a rock spring. They reached this spring without at first realizing it; searching around for it, Lichtenstein stumbled into a crevice and found a green puddle within. Despite its colour, and although *murr* means 'bitter' in Arabic, the water was quite potable.

As they headed towards their next major objective, the extensive and fully inhabited Kharga Oasis complex, they encountered the formidable barrier of the Abu Moharig, the southern end of the same chain of sand dunes that Almasy had tackled during his foolhardy solo trip to the Bahariya Oasis in 1926. Here the dunes were 90 to 100 feet (30 m.) high and composed of fine, fluid sand of the type used in hourglasses. On the windward side the dunes were gently rippled; the leeward sides were steep and precipitous and between the dunes were hard, flat valleys, growing progressively narrower.

To reach Kharga it was necessary to find the correct valley and break through the leeward side of the dune at its end. After a frustrating hour, trying valley after valley only to be turned back each time by an impenetrable dune wall, Almasy was beginning to feel trapped and filled with 'a dreadful urge to flee'. He climbed on foot to the crest of the highest dune and looked around. From his vantage point he could see that the valley in which the two cars were trapped was blocked only by a narrow sand wall, beyond which stretched a long, winding valley leading in the right compass direction for Kharga.

Returning to his car, Almasy reversed to give himself a

good run at it, then accelerated full tilt at the wall of sand. He hit it at 55 mph (90 kph), sending out huge sprays of sand on each side. Then he was through the wall and rolling down to the firm valley floor on the other side. Lichtenstein followed and as Almasy looked back he saw his friend's car burst through 'like a grenade breaking through the wall of a house'.

The moment of triumphant relief was brief, however. When Almasy confessed as dusk was closing in that he did not know their exact position, Lichtenstein exploded and demanded that they retrace their tracks and pick up the marked trail. From that point, said Lichtenstein, *he* would lead. Almasy was concerned. He thought his friend had become panicky under the strains of the journey and was afraid that his panic would spread to the Sudanese.

When they camped for the night and brewed up some tea he slipped a large bromide into Lichtenstein's mug to calm him and soon the prince fell asleep. Almasy turned on his car's headlights so that he could see to make up his bedroll and in the beam he saw a small white fluttering dot. It was a butterfly. A butterfly out in the desert could only mean that they were very close to the oasis. He called the Sudanese and showed them the butterfly. *Hamdu l'illahai* (God be praised), they exulted.

The butterfly must, indeed, have seemed a sign from God – to Muslims, as to Christians, analogous to the dove that proclaimed Noah's deliverance from the Flood. And to Almasy's Sudanese servants such expressions of piety would have been far more than ritualized obedience to blind dogma. As an earlier twentieth-century desert traveller had said, such incantations and prayers are 'an instinctive expression of one's innermost self'.

The prayers at night bring serenity and peace. At dawn when new life has suddenly taken possession of the body, one eagerly turns to the Creator to offer humble homage for all the beauty of the world and of life and to seek guidance for the coming day.

At dawn, following the appearance of the butterfly, Almasy also found guidance. Through his binoculars he was able to make out the tops of distant palms: Kharga it was. He, a mollified Prince Ferdinand and their men set off at once for the oasis without pausing for breakfast.

Kharga is the largest of Egypt's five inhabited oasis complexes, an oval depression 185 miles (300 km.) long by 15 miles (24 km.) wide; it lies, north to south, parallel to the Nile Valley and some 150 miles (250 km.) west of it; it is bordered on the west by the Abu Moharig dune belt and on the north and east by a steep escarpment, 1,000 feet (300 m.) high.

Almasy and his party entered the southernmost of Kharga's scattered patches of arable land amid the characteristic slightly sweet oasis smell of rank grass. 'Praised be Allah, who led us safely across the desert,' said Almasy. Then, following ancient custom by which desert travellers would give thanks to their camels on safe arrival, his men turned to the two cars and touched their bonnets with their right hands 'then, as when greeting, put their hands to their hearts'.

The road between Sudan and Egypt, forgotten since the Mahdi uprising, has now been opened again. For the first

time modern transport equipment has crossed the middle
section of the *Darb el Arba'in*.

Passing through green fields and groves of date palms,
they reached Kharga's southernmost village, Ein Wah,
where they were welcomed by its incredulous inhabitants.

After partaking of a welcoming feast they drove 75 miles
(120 km.) north to the main settlement, Kharga village,
where they were greeted by the governor of the oasis. Fresh
supplies of petrol, ordered in advance by radio from Wadi
Halfa, awaited them. From the governor's office they sent
telegrams to the Egyptian and Sudanese authorities to advise
of their safe arrival and to cancel plans for a possible aerial
search.

But their journey was not done yet. Assiut was another
150 miles to the north and the guide assigned to them
by the oasis governor warned that the Darb el Arba'in
would be completely impassable from Kharga on; it passed
through ravines so strewn with boulders that even camels
would have to be led through individually. The alternative
ways out were by an old caravan trail leading due east, or
along the track of a narrow gauge railway climbing north
up the escarpment to the Nile Plateau. Almasy decided to
exit via the rail track: the weekly train was not due for
another day.

It was a hazardous drive, bumping over the sleepers
in the dark, along the edges of dizzying ravines, and 'the
shivers ran through my back several times' before they
reached the safety of the plateau at daybreak. Henceforward
it was a straight run to Assiut, from where the main road
would take them swiftly back to Cairo, following the river.

Almasy had successfully completed the first crossing by automobile of the mid-section of the Darb el Arba'in. Others would follow.

Chapter 5

The first serious attempt to breach the uncharted immensity of the Libyan Desert had been made in 1874 by the German adventurer Gerhard Rohlfs. As a former member of the French Foreign Legion, he was familiar with the western Sahara but the even more forbidding eastern Sahara was unknown to him. To explore and map it represented a challenge he could not resist when he was invited to lead an expedition sponsored by the Kaiser's foreign ministry and financed by the Egyptian government.

Rohlfs's first objective was to get from Dakhla Oasis to Kufra Oasis, some 380 miles (610 km.) to the west, a stronghold of the xenophobic Zuwaiya tribe which no European had ever seen. Leading an extensive camel train, Rohlfs found his way barred by range upon range of giant sand dunes, running northwest to southeast and parallel to each other – the Great Sand Sea. After days of struggle, Rohlfs was forced to give up the attempt and, to save his men and animals from death by thirst, he turned around and struck north along a hard-surfaced lane between the dunes towards Siwa.

On the way out his party was astonished to encounter a light localized rainfall – the first, said the local Bedouin, in thirty years – on the eastern edge of the Sand Sea. Rohlfs promptly named the spot Regenfeld (Rain-field) on the map he was preparing and moved on, somewhat refreshed. By the time his men and camels reached Siwa they had been on the march for thirty-six days.

Five years later Rohlfs set out again for Kufra, leading another officially sponsored expedition which started from Tripoli. On the way he ran into interference from the suspicious Zuwaiya who relented only after the forceful intervention of the Ottoman governor of Benghazi. He held a number of Zuwaiya sheikhs hostage until they agreed to let Rohlfs proceed, with Zuwaiya guides to help him reach his destination. He got there, but only just. On arrival at Kufra, after a five-day, 275-mile trek from the last water source at Jalo, Rohlfs's party was attacked by the local tribesmen and would almost certainly have been slaughtered but for the timely arrival of a messenger from their spiritual and temporal overlord, the Grand Senussi Sayed Idris, telling them of the deal he had struck with the Ottomans. Rohlfs beat a hasty retreat back to Jalo and Tripoli, leaving behind his scientific equipment, notes and sketch maps.

The next attempt to reach Kufra was made in 1920 – by which time imperialist Italy had replaced Libya's former Ottoman rulers – by an Oxford-educated Egyptian civil servant and future governor of the Egyptian royal household, Ahmed Mohammed Hassanein Bey. He was accompanied by Rosita Forbes, a daring and enterprising young English divorcee and travel writer (shades of Lady Mary Wortley Montagu)* who joined Hassanein's caravan posing

* 1689–1762, author of *Letters of the Right Honourable Lady M—y W—y M—u. Written during her Travels in Europe, Asia and Africa* (edited by John Cleland), London, 1767.

as 'Khadija', the daughter of a wealthy Egyptian and a Circassian slave girl. She had a camera hidden under her veil. It is not clear whether Hassanein knew her real identity when they linked up or whether they subsequently became lovers. It would not be surprising if they did. Both were in their late twenties, he dashingly handsome, she bewitching. She was also ruthlessly ambitious and if their quite separate accounts of their journey together give no hint of the nature of their relationship, that is not surprising either: in her book she dismissed him as a mere assistant and Hassanein, being an honourable man, would not have dreamed of responding in kind or of tarnishing her reputation.

With the approval of the Italians and of Sayed Idris, and accompanied by a Senussi escort, they reached Kufra to find a sandy, rose-red valley bounded on the east by striped sandstone cliffs and dotted by lakes and palm groves. On the instructions of Sayed Idris they were allowed to stay (in separate rooms) as guests of the Senussi Brotherhood in Taj, where 'Khadija' was even allowed to make a pilgrimage to the tomb of Idris's father, the revered Sayed el Mahdi. But when they went on to Jof, the principal town of the oasis and hub of four traditional caravan routes, the suspicious locals threatened their lives and the Brothers warned them to leave quickly and in case of ambush to take a different route from the one they had come in by.

They took his advice, making a four-hundred-mile trek over a little-travelled desert track to Jaghbub, the northern headquarters of the Brotherhood. After a three-day rest there they travelled on to Siwa, across the frontier in Egypt, where Hassanein fell off his camel and broke his collarbone.

He and Rosita were lucky to be picked up by a patrol of the Egyptian Camel Corps and shepherded to safety.

While Hassanein was recuperating from his fracture Rosita travelled on to Cairo, where she was feted at the British High Commission, pursued by male admirers (including the Camel Corps commander, Colonel de Lancey Forth) and hounded by journalists and publishers' representatives. She sold her hastily written account to Cassell in London* and Doubleday in New York and then quit Cairo for Turkey, claiming disingenuously her intention to 'find freedom from being in love as well as to run away from being "famous"'. Eventually returning to London, she found herself even more famous. She was swamped with invitations to speak at luncheons and dinners given in her honour and even summoned to meet King George V and Queen Mary at Buckingham Palace. Later – and by now married once more, to Colonel Arthur McGrath, a handsome military intelligence officer – she went on to mainland Europe, where the Dutch and French geographical societies each awarded her a gold medal.

Amid all this approbation Hassanein remained virtually unacknowledged, except as a footnote in her book, and, so far as the headline-hungry Rosita was concerned, forgotten. He, meanwhile, did his best to extract the utmost scientific benefit from their joint venture. Having been equipped with only basic instruments (an aneroid barometer to measure heights above sea level and a prismatic compass for direction finding), he had been unable to make rigorous

* *The Secret of the Sahara: Kufara*. See Bibliography.

observations. But he did enough to enable Dr John Ball, head of the Egyptian Desert Survey Department, to draw a map pinpointing Kufra's position for the first time. Then Hassanein set off into the desert again to look for more of the 'lost oases' of legend.

For his part, Almasy, having conquered the Forty Days Road, was more than ever determined to find Zerzura. In the 1920s and 1930s its discovery was the ambition of adventurers from many countries. The reality of its existence had been intensely debated in the pages of the Royal Geographical Society's influential and learned *Geographical Journal* and Almasy – despite his protestations that 'I never attempted records, never sought being first' – was intent on leading the first expedition to locate it.

In an odd way, the search for Zerzura seems like a metaphor for the search for the elusive Almasy himself. Bagnold might have had the Hungarian quasi-count in mind when he wrote: 'No sooner is a hopefully reliable piece of evidence found which would appear to tie it down to some definite spot than another account transforms it into an obvious fairy story, or snatches it away to dangle it, an enticing carrot, a long way farther off.'

The most colourful 'fairy story' about Zerzura was to be found in *The Book of Hidden Pearls*, a magical work by an anonymous thirteenth-century Arab author:

In the city of Wardahaba, situated behind the citadel of el Suri, you will see palms, vines and springs. Penetrate into the wadi and pursue your way up it; you will find another wadi running westward between two mountains. From this last wadi starts a road which will lead you to the city of Zerzura, of which you will find the door closed; this city is white like a pigeon, and on the door of it is carved a bird. Take with your hand the key in the beak of the bird, then open the door of the city. Enter, and there you will find great riches, also the king and queen sleeping in their castle. Do not approach them, but take the treasure.

The first reference by a European is in a book by Sir John Gardner Wilkinson, published in 1835. He located Zerzura 'about five days west [by camel] of the road from el Hez to Farfara' and describes it as an oasis 'abounding in palms, with springs and some ruins of uncertain date'.

The inhabitants are blacks, and many of them have been carried off at different times by the Moghrebins for slaves . . . It is supposed that the blacks who invaded Farfara some years ago, and kidnapped a great number of the inhabitants, were from this Oasis . . . By another account Zerzoora is only two or three days due west from Dakleh, beyond which is another wadee; then a second abounding in cattle; then Gebabo and Tazerbo; and beyond these is Wadee Rebeeana.

What made this account seem especially compelling to Almasy's generation was that it mentioned place names – such as 'Tazerbo', 'Gebabo' and 'Rebeeana' – that were unknown to European geographers of Wilkinson's time, but were all located in and around the Kufra Oasis.

As we have seen, the Zerzura legend was much on the mind of European travellers of the late nineteenth century:

Murray's *Guide to Egypt* published in 1896 gives no fewer than four possible locations for the lost oasis and in the early twentieth century pioneer explorers, such as Colonel de Lancey Forth and W. K. Harding-King, a Sudan administration official, were told various stories by various Bedouin whom they encountered on their treks by camel in the Libyan Desert.

Several of these stories mentioned palms and ruins; others spoke of flocks of small birds and, indeed, the Arabic word *zarzura* does mean a small bird. Further legends said the city was guarded by *djinns* who, on the approach of strangers, whipped up a sandstorm to hide the city from view.

All these accounts and legends appeared to locate Zerzura somewhere among the giant dunes of the Sand Sea but after Prince Kemal el Din's discovery of the Gilf Kebir in the late 1920s the would-be discoverers' attentions switched to its plateau, which was high enough to attract a very occasional fall of rain, creating temporary 'rain oases' rather than the more usual artesian oases formed in the desert's giant, wind-scooped depressions.

Although modern geographers and ethnographers of course scoffed at the more fanciful aspects of the Zerzura myth, it seemed quite likely to have a basis in reality, however flimsy. The 'black giants', for example, who supposedly inhabited the oasis, could well be non-Arab, dark-skinned Tibou raiders from the Tibesti Mountains to the southwest; their strange tongue has been likened by some to the squeaking of bats, as told in one of the legendary accounts.

By the 1930s, the lure of the 'lost oasis' had attracted

many romantics and adventurers in addition to Almasy, Bagnold and the other members of the 'Zerzura Club', an entirely informal group of like-minded desert enthusiasts without premises, rules or regulations, beyond an abiding interest in the fabled oasis and an obligation to attend an annual dinner at the Café Royal in London's Regent Street. Among the Zerzura Club's members – though he was never recorded as having attended a meeting – was the British Army lieutenant Orde Wingate, who would achieve fame during World War II as the founder and leader of the Chindit jungle fighters. In 1933, having completed a tour of duty with the Sudan Defence Force, he decided to spend his leave in search of Zerzura and was advised by his mentor and cousin, Sir Reginald Wingate, a former High Commissioner in Egypt, to link up with Almasy. 'It may be a question of life and death,' Sir Reginald wrote, '. . . and I am inclined to think that it might be more advantageous for you and your future to join this Expedition rather than go off on your own.'

But the young Wingate was essentially a loner and, although a notable innovator in matters military, he was a traditionalist when it came to desert travel. He too considered the motor car to be an uncouth intruder into the desert silences and opted to go by camel. Setting out from Dakhla Oasis with thirteen camels and four Bedouin to drive them, he spent five gruelling weeks in a search which yielded little beyond a few animal and bird bones and a prehistoric flint tool. Patrick Clayton, a topographer with the Egyptian Desert Survey Department, encountered him heading back to Dakhla, pushing a home-made mileometer

– a stick with a bicycle wheel attached – to verify his distance travelled.

Despite his failure to find any trace of Zerzura, Wingate was not downcast. 'No one, going forth in the spirit of adventure, has found more joy and delight in the fulfilment of his enterprise than I did in the failure of mine,' he would write. He did not mention whether he had revised his opinion as to the merits of the camel versus the motor car.

Chapter 6

In April 1932 Almasy was exploring the unknown south-western side of the Gilf Kebir in the company of Pat Clayton and two other Englishmen — Wing Commander Hugh Penderel, a World War I fighter ace on leave from the Royal Air Force in Egypt, and Lieutenant Sir Robert Clayton-East-Clayton (no relation to Pat Clayton), a wealthy and adventurous twenty-four-year-old baronet, on leave from the Royal Navy.* Like Almasy and Penderel, he was a qualified pilot.

The expedition had at its disposal three Ford Model A cars, equipped with giant balloon tyres, a 30-cwt. truck, three Sudanese drivers and a cook, and a patched-up De Havilland Tiger Moth biplane named *Rupert* after the popular cartoon bear in the *Daily Express*. *Rupert* was the property of Clayton-East-Clayton, who had bought it 'as is' from a brother officer, who had been far from the proverbial one careful owner. 'His treatment of the machine,' said a mutual friend, 'had not been gentle.'

Clayton-East-Clayton had heard about the Zerzura legend during a dinner conversation with friends one night and, as one of them would later relate, 'his imagination

*On succeeding to the title on the death of his father the young baronet had added two hyphenates to his surname to differentiate himself from another Sir Robert Clayton.

took fire'. He promptly asked for and was granted six months' leave on half-pay from the navy and went off to Hungary to meet Almasy, who he had been told was the man to see.

To Almasy the young British baronet and his aircraft must have seemed the answer to a prayer. He had lost his own plane, also a Tiger Moth, the year before in an ill-fated venture with a Hungarian friend, Count Nandor Zichy. Flying from Hungary via Turkey, they had encountered a violent sandstorm over Syria and crash-landed near Antioch. The plane was a write-off, its occupants initially reported dead by the Syrian press. Miraculously, however, they escaped serious injury, only to find that the other members of their planned expedition, waiting for them in Cairo, had left on hearing reports of their death, taking the expedition's funds with them.

Abandoned and penniless, Almasy and Zichy hitched a lift on a steamer to Marseilles and made their way overland to Budapest. It was one of the lowest points of Almasy's career. Deeply demoralized, he remained determined to find some way – and some other funding – to continue his search for Zerzura. But he encountered only 'disappointments and rebuttals, among which the cold voices at home hurt the most'. The triple-barrelled Sir Robert proved to be the providential antidote to that hurt. He and Almasy soon agreed on a joint venture, at Sir Robert's expense, and plans were made to leave for Egypt as soon as possible. In the rush of preparations, the impetuous young baronet found time to get married in London and a fortnight later he and his bride, formerly Dorothy Durrant, the sculptress daughter of a well-connected High Church vicar, were on their way to Cairo in *Rupert*.

There, Sir Robert met up with Almasy and had extensive repairs carried out on the plane – 'sewn up with bootlaces', as he would say – at RAF Heliopolis. His spirited bride, a striking blonde,★ known to her friends as 'Peter', was keen to join the trek into the desert, but her husband and the other men vetoed the idea, citing lack of space, shortage of supplies and the inherent dangers of the expedition. Seething with disappointment, she was left behind in Cairo with Pat Clayton's wife, Ellie.

While Almasy and Pat Clayton drove south to Kharga, Sir Robert and Penderel flew there in *Rupert*, to await the arrival by train of 16,000 litres of aviation fuel they had bought in Cairo. When Almasy and Pat Clayton arrived the four of them linked up to take the petrol 330 miles across the desert by lorry and establish a series of fuel, food and water dumps and landing strips along the southern and western edges of the Gilf escarpment.

Once the dumps had been set up, Pat Clayton drove north with one Sudanese to check out some important landmarks, Penderel and Sir Robert returned to Kharga to collect *Rupert*, and Almasy stayed behind alone to wait for them at Bir Messaha, a Survey Department well in the middle of a vast, featureless sandy plain. No sooner had his companions driven off than Almasy began to have misgivings about being entirely alone in the desert, three

★ The *Daily Express*'s William Hickey column had noted that she adorned her fair hair with then-fashionable dark streaks.

hundred miles from the nearest habitation, for the next four or five days – a task he had accepted 'without any forethought, yielding to a momentary urge'.

A moment of near-panic seized him. Would he be able unaided, to lift the heavy wooden cover of the well? And if so, had he the strength to winch up the cable carrying a 60-litre steel tank from the water level 100 feet below? Carefully, standing on the stone surround of the well-mouth and constantly checking his balance, Almasy lifted the lid inch by inch. With equal caution he disconnected the steel tank from its cable and substituted an empty 5-litre petrol can, all the while keeping an eye open for scorpions, a number of which had made their home under the shade of the well's wooden roof.

Then he lowered the petrol can and winched it back up, not certain till he recovered it whether he had gone down deep enough. He had, and he repeated the process three more times, ensuring that he had sufficient water to last until the others returned. In his tent that night he realized he was not entirely alone. A tiny jerboa, or desert rat, emerged timidly from hiding, apparently looking for food. How did such animals survive out there, Almasy wondered. He placed a date in the circle of light from his paraffin lamp. Cautiously, the jerboa emerged to snatch it and carry it off to its lair, clutched between chin and forepaws. The next night it took a date from Almasy's hand.

During his lonely wait Almasy slept, read and wrote his diary in the heat of the day, emerging at night to wander in the moonlight. 'Truly,' he philosophized, 'the noble tranquillity of the desert brings us closer to the mind of the Almighty.' At noon on the fourth day he awoke from a doze to feel on his skin – rather than to hear – the approach of *Rupert*. Dashing outside, he guided the Tiger Moth in to the prepared landing strip with a hand mirror. It had been 'the worst flight I have ever done or wish to do', Clayton-East-Clayton would recall.

As the sun got higher the tracks became invisible. I had to keep my eyes glued on the ground the whole time; lifting them only for a second meant losing the tracks for good. What with the terrible glare and the intense concentration needed I lost all idea of height, position and speed. My head began to swim and I had an almost unbearable longing to dive the machine into the ground and end it all.

At Bir Messaha he and Penderel 'just lay in the [shade of the] winch and sweated' until they and Almasy were joined by Pat Clayton, returning by car from the western flank of the Gilf.

The nightmarish flight from Kharga was only the first act of Sir Robert's gruelling introduction to the hazards and hardships of desert travel. A few days later, having left Almasy and Pat Clayton behind at a camp at the southwest corner of the Gilf, under twin hills they named Peter and Paul, he and Penderel set off on what they thought would be a brief mapping mission with the three Sudanese and two cars. The visibility was bad and no landmarks could be seen. To make matters worse they ran into a sandstorm and it became necessary to ration both petrol and water. They were lost and they realized that Almasy and Pat Clayton would have very little chance of finding them with the one car they had left behind in camp.

> There was only the slightest chance of our ever coming out of the business alive [wrote Sir Robert] and I must say I found myself a bigger coward than I thought I was . . . I thought of tankards of beer, England and all the wet things one does think about on these occasions and I wondered why I had spent a lot of money to go and die in the desert.

The next morning they sent three Sudanese on foot to look for a landmark – specifically a cairn which, according to their maps, stood atop a small hill to the north. After several hours the trio returned to say there was no cairn on the hill. The two Englishmen decided to drive north anyway, but their petrol ran out at the base of the hill. They climbed it on foot and found that there *was* a cairn on the top, after all: 'The wretched Arabs had tired before reaching the hill and reported wrongly.'

Knowing now that their camp was only fifteen miles away, they sent the Sudanese to bring back a can of petrol and settled down for the night by their car, vowing never again to trust an Arab guide, however good. 'Then we brewed a cup of tea from the radiator water. Although the water was darker than the tea I have never tasted a drink nearly so good. The mixture of oil, rust and dirt only made it nicer.'

Reunited at their camp the next day, the four explorers took it in turns to make systematic surveys by land and by air of the Gilf escarpment and its plateau, which they noted was deeply scarred by ancient but long dried-up water-courses. The presence of these wadis convinced Almasy not only that the region must once have been green and fertile but that there might still be a rain oasis in the vicinity, either at the foot of the Gilf or somewhere on its vast plateau. This was mainly barren but relieved here and there by sparse patches of vegetation and struggling acacia trees, encouraging Almasy to believe that the plateau might well contain among its hidden valleys the legendary, long-lost Zerzura.

After several days of hazardous, 'intensely interesting' but inconclusive reconnaissance flights in the radio-less *Rupert* over the Gilf, Sir Robert, for one, became increasingly apprehensive that the rocky plateau 'looked too bad for a forced landing . . . and almost impossible of access [up the escarpment] by rescuing cars'. To add to their problems, when Almasy checked their reserves of water he found these were running dangerously low. They would have to abandon their search if they could not be replenished.

But where would they find water? Almasy suggested Kufra Oasis, 125 miles (200 km.) northwest, across the border into Libya. His three British companions did not like the idea. The Sand Sea lay in between their camp and Kufra and no one had ever reached the oasis from the east. Besides, Kufra was a war zone and occupied by the Italians in the course of a long-running campaign to subdue the recalcitrant Senussi of Cyrenaica.

But Almasy was confident that he could get across the sand dunes and moreover that, as a Hungarian, he would be welcomed by the Italian garrison where his British companions, two of them serving officers, might not. After debating long and heatedly into the night, Almasy won the reluctant agreement of his companions. He left the next morning with the three Sudanese drivers in two vehicles. Against expectations, the crossing to Kufra was relatively uneventful, much of the way proving to be by firm-surfaced corridors between dunes. Nevertheless, when Almasy reached the southernmost village of the extensive Kufra Oasis complex he found the inhabitants unwilling to believe that he had come from across the Egyptian frontier. No one had reached Kufra from that direction before.

Chapter 7

Although Almasy was the first outsider to reach Kufra from the Egyptian side of the frontier, the Italians had been able the year before to seize the oasis complex by bringing in and merging three military columns from the north, west and east to launch a sudden attack with close air support.

It was a remarkable feat of logistics and force co-ordination, the climax of a nineteen-year campaign to subdue the whole of what is present-day Libya in the teeth of stubborn Senussi resistance.

The unification of Italy, occurring as late as 1860, had left the Italians without an overseas empire and they were determined as a matter of national pride to catch up with their colonialist European neighbours, such as Britain, France, Holland and Portugal.

An ill-considered attempt to invade and occupy Abyssinia in 1896 had ended in fiasco when a ragtag defending force decisively routed the Italians at Adowa, on the Red Sea coast. In 1912 the Italians felt strong enough to try their hand at empire-building once more, this time by seizing Tripolitania and Cyrenaica, south across the Mediterranean, from the enfeebled Ottoman Empire. They invaded over the vocal protests of home-grown liberals and socialists, among them a young left-wing journalist named Benito Mussolini.

But ten years later, by which time the socialist Mussolini had transformed himself into the fascist dictator *Il Duce*, he was all in favour of creating a new Roman Empire, of which Libya – once a province of the old Roman Empire – would be a prestigious component, for historical as well as commercial and territorial reasons. Even before the rise of Mussolini and his *fascisti*, the Senussi had never embraced the concept of *civis Romanus sum* and continued to give the black-shirted occupiers a hard time. They were what we would nowadays call Islamic fundamentalists – some might add 'terrorists' – with an inbred contempt for 'infidels' or for any outsiders, a strong sense of their own identity, an equally strong streak of cruelty and a well-honed talent for guerrilla warfare.

For ten years following the Italian invasion they harried the intruders without restraint, under the leadership of their veteran guerrilla chief, Omar el Mukhtar. In 1922, by which time the Italians had occupied a string of oases across the northern part of Cyrenaica, the rebels' spiritual and temporal leader, Idris the Grand Senussi, signed a treaty with the Italians which, in return for a cessation of hostilities, guaranteed his continued control over the Senussis' principal southern stronghold, Kufra.

An uneasy peace – punctuated by sporadic raids by the recalcitrant Omar el Mukhtar invariably followed by ruthless Italian retaliation* – lasted for almost a decade. Finally, the Italians decided to put a permanent end to this 'nuis-

* An estimated twenty thousand Senussi captives died in Italian prison camps and the Bedouin population of Libya was halved.

ance'. In January 1931 three columns of Italian troops with armoured cars and close air support converged on Kufra in perfect coordination, one column traversing dune fields that were previously considered impassable. Suddenly and without warning they attacked. The Senussi, fierce and warlike though they were, were totally demoralized by this ruthless display of fascist will, logistic brio and modern military technology. Panicked by air strikes – and without even delaying to stock up adequately with food and water for themselves and their camels – an estimated two thousand Senussi men, women and children fled into the desert, relentlessly bombed and machine-gunned by pursuing Italian warplanes. There, the great majority of the refugees perished, either quickly by bullets and high explosives or slowly from thirst, hunger and exposure.

In fascist Italy this feat of colonialist bravura was received with wild public acclaim. Field Marshal Pietro Badoglio, the governor-general of Libya, and General Rodolfo Graziani, its military commander-in-chief, flew down to Kufra for the ceremonial raising of the Italian flag and the unveiling of a jut-jawed bust of *Il Duce* in the officers' mess at Jof, Kufra's scruffy little principal town. Serious native resistance to the Italian presence was effectively at an end throughout Libya.

By the time Almasy reached Kufra, fourteen months after these events, the Italians had firmly established themselves over the oasis and its six thousand remaining inhabitants, many of them Tibou and others who had been subservient to the dominant Zuwaiya. Kufra's military governor, Major Ottavio Rolle, went out of his way to give Almasy the red–carpet treatment. He proudly showed the unexpected visitor around his bailiwick, beaming when children rushed to greet them with the straight-arm fascist salute – *il saluto Romano* – and treating him to the luxury of a warm bath and a good lunch with his subordinate officers at Jof.

Almasy was suitably impressed. In his subsequent account of his desert adventures he blamed 'the fanatic xenophobia' of the Senussi for 'obliging' the Italians to take the oasis in what he admiringly – and, in strictly military terms, justifiably – called a 'superbly conducted' operation. What a pity it was, he thought, that the Senussi had not been wise enough to placate the Italians, avert war and thus maintain the isolation and mystery of their remote fiefdom.

Isolated it certainly was, though covering several hundred square miles and at the confluence of four traditional caravan routes. 'It is difficult to exaggerate the loneliness of the oasis,' wrote Kennedy Shaw.

In English geographical equivalents, taking Kufra as London, the nearest place where you could be sure of finding another human being who would give you a drink of water were Rebiana (Salisbury), Bzema (Coventry), or Tazerbo (Liverpool), while to be certain of a glass of beer you must go to Benghazi (Berlin).

Almasy's overall impression of the Italian occupation was that the people of Kufra were far happier under Italian rule than might have been expected. As for Rolle himself, Almasy thought him 'broad-minded and clever' – a soldier, judge, architect and agronomist rolled into one, stern but fatherly towards his subjects.

The night before Almasy's departure to rejoin his expedition, this fascist paragon gave a mini-banquet in his guest's honour, attended by six of his subordinate officers and the garrison physician, while Mussolini's bust looked benevolently down from a high pedestal. Almasy felt 'warm emotions' when Rolle proposed a toast to Hungary. And when Almasy drove off at dawn with his three Sudanese they took with them as the gift of the Italians 250 litres of water, several baskets of fresh eggs and vegetables, four live chickens and a case of Chianti.

On his return to camp – henceforth to be renamed Chianti Camp – Almasy was greeted by his companions with back slaps and the news that on a reconnaissance flight over the Gilf they had spotted a wadi that was 'quite possibly Zerzura'.

It seemed to be about 30 or 40 kilometres [19 or 25 miles] long and as far as we could see filled with trees. This was intensely interesting. We would have liked to fly right to the end, but the thought of a forced landing in that broken, rocky country was too much for us.

They calculated that the exit to this wadi would be about sixty miles to the north along the base of the escarpment and tried to find it by car, but after three days' search and using up most of their petrol they had to admit defeat. 'Old man Wadi has beaten us!' wrote Sir Robert. 'There is no more juice and it must be the return journey tomorrow. No wonder he is called the lost oasis.'

Pat Clayton's verdict was more upbeat:

We consider it certain that this *wadi* is one of those whose existence and occasional occupation by Arabs has given rise to the legends . . . It derives its water from the occasional rainfall on the Gilf Kebir plateau . . . Water would almost certainly be available in such a *wadi* for a year or two after rain.

The next day they set out on an uneventful return trip to Kharga, feeling the expedition had been far from a failure and reckoning that another expedition would be needed to build on what they had discovered so far. They arrived at Kharga in time for Almasy and Pat Clayton to catch the weekly train to Cairo, while the others flew back in *Rupert*. A few miles out of Kharga, Almasy had the chance to display his mechanic's skills when the train's engine broke down – the only mechanical mishap of the entire trip.

Back in Cairo, Almasy found he was by no means alone in his admiration for the Italian capture and occupation of Kufra. In London, *The Times* described the military operation as 'brilliant', reporting approvingly that when the Italians captured thirty-nine of the fleeing Senussi 'seven were recognized as traitors and spies and were shot on the spot'.

And when the seventy-two-year-old Senussi guerrilla leader, Omar el Mukhtar, was captured in September 1931 and hanged the next day in front of twenty thousand prisoners brought in by the Italians to 'note, mark and inwardly digest' the lesson of his fate, *The Times* observed with Olympian detachment that 'his execution was the natural consequence of his breach of the truce of 1929 [sic]★'.

The complaisance of the British Establishment notwith-standing, Almasy's warm endorsement of the Italian victory and occupation gave rise to suspicion in both Whitehall and Cairo that he must be working for Rome. And, after all, there was an ideological affinity between the Hungarian and Italian regimes.

But, as with almost everything connected with Almasy, the truth was not nearly so clear-cut. He was by no means alone in his admiration of Mussolini and his blackshirts – even Winston Churchill had spoken well of them. Almasy's enthusiasm for the capture of Kufra could have been no more than an expression of political naivety by a royalist conservative, predisposed by background and upbringing (no doubt reinforced by Major Rolle's hospitality) to think indulgently of Rome's imperial ambitions.

On the other hand, Almasy must surely have known from Pat Clayton – who had been instrumental in rescuing many of the Kufra refugees from the desert the year before – and from one of his Sudanese servants, Abu Fudeil, who had married a refugee woman – just how desperate the plight of the Senussi had been, and just how ruthless the assault of the Italians.

It was several days before news of that assault had reached the Egyptian authorities on their side of the frontier and several months more before Almasy learned at first hand

★ By contrast, the Egyptian press published 'detailed and terrible accounts of the alleged Italian atrocities' and in a riot outside the Italian consulate in Cairo a gendarme was killed and several injured.

from Effendi Abd el Rahman, police chief of the Dhakla Oasis, of the Egyptians' urgent if belated attempts to rescue the surviving refugees.

By the time Rahman heard of their plight they had been wandering in the desert for three weeks. Reading from his notes of the rescue operation, he told Almasy how he and the oasis doctor, commandeering the handful of cars available, had driven out from Mut, Dhakla's principal town, on the evening of 23 February 1931, followed by a detachment of policemen on camels carrying a large supply of water.

At nine in the evening we found a group of Senussi lying lifeless in the desert. They were 21 in all, men, women and children . . . At six in the evening [of the 25th] . . . we found four women, six girls and the same number of [boy] children. The women rejoiced when they saw us with such weak voices that we hardly heard them . . . They were so weak and their voices so faint that we all had tears in our eyes . . . At seven we found [a man] with three women, three girls and a seven year old boy. The condition of these was no better . . . At 40 past seven we found 20 men, 19 women and 22 children. They were in terrible shape . . . It was a miserable sight when a mother grabbed the water canteen from my hand as I was giving it to her dying child . . .

And so on, until 8 March, by which time the Dakhla police chief and his assistants had saved 302 men, women and children, and buried sixty-three, leaving hundreds of undiscovered dead in the desert.

After hearing Rahman's account Almasy told him he had been assured by Rolle that the surviving refugees would be

1–3. *Top*, the Almasy children. Left to right, Janos, Gyorgina and Laszlo on the lake at Castle Borostyanko, *c.* 1903; *above left*, the Almasy children with their mother Ilona, *c.* 1903; *right*, Gyorgy Almasy with his two sons, Laszlo (left) and Janos (right), 1916

4. Laszlo Almasy in Khartoum during his East African safari, 1929

5. Almasy and his travelling companion Prince Ferdinand of Lichtenstein on their 1929 safari

6. Two stripped-down Ford pick-ups followed by a Citroën half-track negotiating the down slope of a dune near Jebel Uweinat

7. Ralph Bagnold and companions dig out a Ford Model A stuck in soft sand, c. 1932

8. Robert Clayton-East-Clayton and Hugh Penderel in the shadow of a giant mushroom rock south of Gilf Kebir, 1932

9, 10. Robert Clayton-East-Clayton and his wife Dorothy. They were the glamorous couple whose brief lives were linked with Almasy's

11. Kharga, Egypt's largest oasis. Haven for the Zuweiya refugees fleeing the Italian assault on Kufra

12. Almasy, breakfasting en route to the Gilf Kebir, eyes the chickens that will provide his future meals. Note the fat balloon tyres on the Ford giving more traction on loose sand

13. Gilf Kebir plateau photographed from *Rupert*, 1932

14. Hugh Penderel shelters from the sun under *Rupert*'s wing

15. The Great Sand Sea merging into the northern edge of the
Gilf Kebir

16. Almasy (seated) between Hans Rhotert and Professor Frobenius
during their search for the cave paintings

17. Ahmed Hassanein Bey photographed one of his men
drawing water at Ain Doua, near Jebel Uweinat

allowed to return to Kufra at the Italians' expense. Their flight had been 'madness', Almasy insisted. 'There was no need for this disorganized escape . . . They were offered an amnesty if they laid down their arms without a fight . . . [The Italians] threw down proclamations from aeroplanes before occupying the oasis.' 'But it all happened *because* of the aeroplanes,' insisted the police chief, to which Almasy replied: 'Such is war.'

Pat Clayton had reported to the British authorities on *his* part in the rescue of the Kufra refugees. He was out in the unmapped desert south of the Gilf Kebir, on a triangulation mission for the Survey Department when, by sheer chance and without knowing of the Italian offensive, he came across a family of ten 'in a starving and pitiable condition'. They had walked from Kufra and had not eaten for days.

The women's feet were so raw that they could only crawl on hands and knees. They were scared too, as our Fords were the first cars they had ever seen. I picked them up . . . but feared some of them would die before we reached my main camp 210 miles away.

In his official report, the taciturn Clayton omitted to explain exactly how he had found the ten refugees and how he had managed to transport them to safety. It had been an extraordinary coincidence. Before leaving Wadi Halfa on his survey mission Clayton had run into Bagnold who told him where to find a vehicle with a broken differential that he (Bagnold) had been forced to abandon near Uweinat, together with a hidden petrol dump. From Cairo, Bagnold had sent on to Clayton at Wadi Halfa all the spare parts and new tyres needed to get the abandoned vehicle going again.

Sure enough, Clayton found the car – and, to his astonishment, the pathetic refugee family of ten, sitting around it, as if believing that this disabled foreign machine might somehow save them. With Clayton's help, it did. As Bagnold would later record:

> After a great struggle and continued use of heavy sledge-hammers they got the back axle apart; the broken parts were replaced by the new ones and the car was made whole again. He [Clayton] packed the ten thin almost dead bodies into it and dispatched it along with one of his native drivers direct to Wadi Halfa. Here the pathetic cargo was rushed into hospital, where the majority recovered.

Having seen this group off to safety, Clayton began searching the desert for other survivors. During the next couple of weeks he and his Sudanese assistants covered some five thousand miles of desert following the tracks of the refugees, who had broken up into small bands. They managed to save thirty-seven more men, women and children and get them to Dakhla.

Bill Kennedy Shaw, who happened to be in Dakhla at the time, reported later: 'The total number of Arabs reaching Dakhla was about 300. The first arrivals must have covered 420 miles without water over arid desert, a feat of endurance which can have few parallels in the history of desert travel.'

For their efforts, both Clayton and the Dakhla police chief received medals from King Fuad of Egypt. And although Clayton in no way tried to dramatize his humanitarian achievement and was generally careful not to express his distaste for the Italians' behaviour in public, he remained in bad odour with the *fascisti*. For years, they regarded him as 'a dubious person who continually runs down Italy'.

Chapter 8

After his triumphant excursion to Kufra the remainder of 1932 was a trying year for Almasy. Perennially hard up, like so many younger sons of the European landed gentry, he lost his job and regular income when the Steyr motor company laid him off in the global depression that followed the Wall Street crash of 1929. Worse was to come for his finances with the deaths, within seven months of each other, of his wealthy young British client, Sir Robert Clayton-East-Clayton, and his even wealthier and more influential Egyptian royal sponsor, Prince Kemal el Din.

Had Kemal wished, he might have been King of Egypt. He was the only son of Sultan Hussein Kemal whom the British put on the throne in 1914 after ousting his pro-German predecessor, Abbas Hilmi. But Hussein was only to rule for three years plus a few days before dying (of natural causes), whereupon Kemal renounced all claims to the throne in favour of his uncle, Fuad.

This came as no surprise. Kemal had made it clear that he had no taste for public life, nor did he believe that there was any satisfaction to be gleaned from sitting on the throne as a puppet of the British. His ruling passions were, in the physical world, desert exploration, and in the spiritual world, Suffism – the mystical belief system which, contrary to Islamic orthodoxy, holds that Muslims should side-

86

line their clergy and build a direct personal relationship with God.

So when he was not praying and meditating in his palace beside the Nile with fellow members of the reclusive Bektashi sect, Kemal was out in the deep desert heading his fleet of custom-built Citroën half-tracks and six-wheelers, mapping the northeastern fringes of the mighty Gilf Kebir and the mountains and gravel plains beyond it to the south.

When ill health curtailed his further desert expeditions in the early 1930s, he compensated by giving generous financial and political support to Almasy's attempts to complete the mapping of the Gilf and to locate Zerzura. To formalize his support Kemal signed Almasy to a three-year contract and, as if to spur him to greater effort, spoke of his plans to persuade his uncle Fuad to found a desert institute. The implication here was that Almasy, who considered himself to be 'at the height of success and recognition', was the obvious choice to head the institute.

But Kemal, like his father before him, had only a short time to live. During one of his final desert expeditions he had contracted an infection in his right leg, which had eventually to be amputated. Then, while on holiday in the South of France in February 1932, he died suddenly of unanticipated complications, aged fifty-eight. He was buried, by his own wish, in the Mokatam Hills overlooking the Nile Valley, the home ground of the Suffi sect of dervishes whose beliefs he shared.

Almasy was in Hungary when he received news of Kemal's death. Mourning the loss of his royal sponsor, he was moved to remark that 'destiny is more cruel than the desert'. Later he would erect a cairn to Kemal's memory in the desert at Regenfeld.

In September of the same year – a few months after his return to England from his desert expedition with Almasy, Penderel, Pat Clayton and *Rupert* – the adventurous Sir Robert Clayton-East-Clayton died at his family home, Hall Place, near Maidenhead. Like Prince Kemal (and eventually Almasy himself) he was a belated victim of the desert. Almost certainly he had returned from Egypt already incubating an infection picked up during the exhausting and debilitating search for Zerzura.

Before falling ill, Sir Robert had mustered the strength to write his lively and refreshingly candid accounts of the expedition for *The Times* and the *Geographical Journal*. But the damage had been done. Soon after publication, he went down with what was diagnosed as acute anterior poliomyelitis, a then incurable condition. And although attended by no fewer than five doctors and put into emergency breathing apparatus – a so-called iron lung – he could not be saved.

He died childless and, being an only son, the baronetcy, created in 1732, died with him. In accordance with his last wishes, his young widow, an accomplished 'A' licence pilot, dropped his ashes over the English Channel from the cockpit of *Rupert*. Six months later she set off again for Egypt, armed with her husband's maps and saying that she was determined to continue the search for Zerzura, from which she had previously been excluded by what might nowadays be termed male chauvinism.

'I am only carrying on my husband's work. We always

did this sort of thing together,' she told a London newspaper, not entirely truthfully. 'I do not think there will be
much danger from the desert tribes and I am not taking a
pistol.'

In Cairo, accompanied by her late husband's fellow
naval officer, Lieutenant Commander Dickie Roundell, she
arranged to join Pat Clayton on his latest Desert Survey
expedition to the Sand Sea. They set up camp on the
western edge of the Gilf escarpment, close to the Libyan
border. Pointedly, it seems, she had made no attempt
to link up with Almasy, whom she had met previously in
Cairo. She and Clayton's wife, Ellie, had both conceived
an aversion to him, having 'immediately detected his homosexual tendencies and his capacity to induce distrust in some
of those who knew him'.

Lady Dorothy publicly declined to shake Almasy's hand
on more than one occasion. As for Ellie Clayton, she too
'simply couldn't stand him', as her son Peter would recall
many years later. It is not at all clear how the two women
were so quick to spot Almasy's sexual orientation. He had
acquired a public reputation as a womanizer on the look-
out for a wealthy wife, but whispered and unsubstantiated
Cairo gossip hinted otherwise, suggesting that he patronized
the 'rough trade' that was readily available in the capital's
back-street bars and boy brothels. (All this, of course, sits
in disconcerting contrast to the fictional relationship of a
robustly heterosexual Almasy and a besotted 'Katharine
Clifton', which is at the heart of *The English Patient*. The
Katharine of novel and screenplay and her husband Geoffrey
are obviously based on the real-life Dorothy and Robert

Clayton–East–Clayton: disregarding hyphenates the sur-
names Clifton and Clayton are almost the same and even
the Tiger Moth *Rupert* appears under the same name.)

Leading a convoy of six Ford cars and lorries, Pat Clayton
set up camp close to the Libyan border on the north-
western edge of the Gilf. From there, he, Roundell and Lady
Dorothy managed to get up to the top of the Gilf, not by
attempting to climb the escarpment which bounds it on the
west, south and east but by approaching from the Sand Sea
to the north, where the dunes merge into the rocky plateau.

While on the plateau they managed to explore a section
of 'the mysterious *wadi*' that Sir Robert and Penderel had
spotted from the air the year before. It was comparatively
well-wooded, mainly by stunted acacias, and it harboured
a good deal of bird and animal life. At one spot they found
the skeletal remains of hundreds of addax, a rare cow-sized
mountain sheep, suggesting that this was the place where
the animals instinctively came to die.

Returning to camp from this sortie via the escarpment,
they nearly came to grief when their car's brakes locked and
they slid wildly down as if on a toboggan. Surviving this
experience convinced them that 'there is no country that
cannot be traversed by a little optimism and a Ford lorry'.

While Lady Dorothy, Roundell and Clayton were
exploring the plateau and western wall of the Gilf, Almásy
and Penderel – on leave again from commanding the RAF's
212 Squadron – were co-leading an expedition on the
eastern side of it. They were accompanied by the Austrian
author and journalist, Richard Bermann, who was to write
an account of the expedition, Laszlo Kadar, a Hungarian

geographer and geologist, and Hans Casparius, the expedition's photographer. In the context of Almasy's later alleged pro-Nazi sympathies, the presence on his expedition of Bermann – and of the apparent friendship between the two men – is perhaps significant.

Bermann, a fifty-year-old bachelor, was a correspondent for the *Berliner Tageblatt*, writing under the name of Arnold Hollriegel. He was vocally left wing and visibly Jewish – a combination unlikely to appeal to a patrician conservative royalist, let alone a proto-Nazi. Yet in his 1934 account of his desert travels, Almasy went out of his way to refer repeatedly to 'my friend Bermann' – pointedly not using his pen-name – as if sending a message that here, at least, was one Hungarian aristocrat who was not racially prejudiced or politically blinkered.*

Neither Almasy's nor Lady Dorothy's expedition succeeded in its objective of pinpointing the legendary lost oasis. And after exhaustive exploration of the Gilf escarpment, from the air and by car, and many of the wadis across the plateau, both teams ended up in the Kufra Oasis, where they were hospitably received by the Italian occupiers. But still the two expeditions never met up: forewarned of Almasy's impending arrival, Lady Dorothy and her party left to drive north in the early morning of the very day that Almasy and his party got there.

From Kufra, she, Roundell and Clayton made a record-setting journey covering the entire length of the Sand Sea

* Bermann fled Austria after the Nazi takeover in 1938 and went to the US where he died during World War II.

to Siwa Oasis, some four hundred miles away as the crow flies, and – intentionally or otherwise – forestalling Almasy, who had ambitions to be the first to complete the same epic drive. '[It was] a feat which would appear barely possible,' she would write, 'but we accomplished it with really very little difficulty.'

Sometimes we would drive along the crests of the dunes and sometimes in the 'streets' between them, and all the time the going was easier than it had been on the east to west trips between Western Camp and Ain Dalla.

Not long after her return to England, the inexhaustible Lady Dorothy set off on another testing expedition, this time to a very different locale: Lapland. But in September 1933, back in England again, she was to meet her death in melodramatic and never fully explained circumstances.

It happened at the Brooklands Aero Club, near Weybridge in Surrey, during a weekend of aircraft and motor car races, a mere five days after her return from Lapland. This time she was piloting her two-seater Spartan Arrow biplane, a hand-made, state-of-the-art aircraft that she had bought brand new only a few months before. Earlier in the day she had gone up in the Arrow with the aero club's chief flight instructor, Max Finlay, to make sure that all was in order before taking part in one of the races. It was common practice to take this precaution before competing and all the Arrow's systems seemed in good working order.

But as the race began a few hours later, and she was picking up speed for take-off, something went horribly wrong. Travelling at about 50 mph (80 kph), the Arrow was seen to swerve to the left and then to the right. Lady Dorothy struggled upright in the open cockpit, fumbled with her safety belt and then, to the horror of onlookers, was seen to jump – or fall – from the speeding plane. She hit the runway just opposite the clubhouse and somersaulted, sustaining massive head injuries. She was pronounced dead within the hour.

By macabre coincidence, the day after her death *The Times* published Lady Dorothy's account of her desert expedition, which had unaccountably been delayed four months in transmission from Cairo. When all the wadis of the Gilf plateau had been visited and the lost oasis had still not been located, she wrote, 'then we shall have narrowed down the Zerzura problem, perhaps to the vanishing point; but until that has been done the lost oasis is still there to be found'.

At the inquest into her death three days later, technical evidence was given that the plane's throttle control rod, governing the speed of the engine's revolutions, was corroded and had broken. But Max Finlay told the coroner that she could quite easily have turned off the engine by putting her hand over the side of the open cockpit and throwing the magneto switch. 'Did she know that?' asked the coroner. 'Oh, yes,' replied Finlay. 'She was an experienced amateur pilot.'

Major Cooper, an expert witness from the Air Ministry, was similarly baffled by Lady Dorothy's failure to reach out and switch off. The plane was quite manageable, even with the control rod broken, he said, and her behaviour was 'extraordinary'. The authoritative aviation magazine *Flight* took the same view: 'It is difficult to explain why the pilot did not resort to the simple remedy of switching off the engine.'

The coroner returned a verdict of 'death by misadventure' – one that seems to leave many questions unanswered. For instance, no evidence was sought as to Lady Dorothy's state of mind as a consequence of her husband's death after only six months of marriage. And although Major Cooper had ascribed the condition of the control rod to corrosion and lack of lubrication, the almost-new plane had reportedly been regularly inspected – and, as we have seen, taken up on a successful test flight that very morning. Also, the Arrow had been kept in a hangar throughout the summer while Lady Dorothy was in Lapland and in no way exposed to the elements.

It is tempting to speculate that a more rigorous inquiry might have returned a rather different verdict. While there is no surviving evidence of her delayed mental or emotional reaction to her husband's tragically early death, it seems reasonable to assume that, in the afterglow of honeymoon, she may well have become deeply despondent. Yet the coroner failed to pursue this line of inquiry. It seems almost as though he was reluctant to venture down a path that might lead to an unwelcome destination – a verdict of 'suicide while the balance of her mind was disturbed'.

It should be remembered that 1930s Britain was a distinctly deferential society. Lady Dorothy's family and her in-laws were from the upper stratum of society and both recently bereaved. Under the circumstances, and given the stigma attached, a verdict of suicide, provoking lurid headlines in the mass-circulation press, might well have seemed to a class-conscious coroner to be insensitive.

On the other hand, it must be said that to jump from a moving plane at take-off does seem an odd way to commit suicide. Far better, surely, to take the plane up a thousand feet or so and then nose-dive into an empty field, rather than risk the lives of innocent spectators on the ground. And to leave a suicide note.

But what explanation other than suicide could there be? Sabotage? A sudden, uncharacteristic panic attack? Or even, as one of her relatives has implausibly suggested, some sinister, long-distance intervention by Almasy himself? All of the above seem even less likely than suicide and so long after the event, when all the trails have gone completely cold, Lady Dorothy's death must remain just another of the mysteries with links to the perplexing life and troubled times of Laszlo Almasy.

Chapter 9

Despite his fixation on the two desert legends – the lost oasis of Zerzura and the lost army of Cambyses – Almasy was about to make a find of scientific and cultural significance that would bring him more celebrity and more controversy than either. This was the discovery of dozens of Stone Age rock paintings on the walls and ceilings of caves along the southern and western fringes of the Gilf Kebir escarpment, perhaps the most intriguing and best known of them the Cave of the Swimming Men.

Almasy was by no means the first explorer to find cave paintings and rock engravings in this area. That honour falls to Ahmed Mohammed Hassanein Bey, the first outsider to get into Kufra. Pushing deeper south beyond the Gilf Kebir by camel and reaching Jebel Uweinat in 1923, Hassanein was intrigued to find what the Tibou called 'a secret valley inhabited by *Jinns* and *Afrits* [spirits]'. Deep inside this 'haunted' wadi he came across a cave decorated by paintings of animals which could only have been known to its inhabitants before the relentless process of desertification began ten thousand years and more ago.

These included 'lions, giraffes and ostriches, all kinds of gazelle and perhaps cows, though many of these were effaced by time . . . ,' wrote Hassanein. And 'although primitive in character they betrayed an artistic hand. The man who drew these outline figures had a decorative sense . . . The pictures were rudely but not unskilfully carved.'

On his return to Cairo Hassanein described his find to Prince Kemal, who trekked south in 1924, at the head of his fleet of half-tracks, to photograph Hassanein's rock pictures and to find more in other caves. In the autumn of 1932, Bagnold also found such paintings in caves at Ain Doua, in the shadow of the 6,000-foot (1,900-m.) Jebel Uweinat, a towering, fortress-like mountain in the then-disputed border region between British-controlled Sudan and Italian-occupied Libya.

These discoveries confirmed what geological observation had already suggested, and more recent satellite evidence has conclusively underscored: that in the distant past, before the desert gradually took over, the region had been criss-crossed by mountain torrents and studded with lakes, giving life to flora and fauna nowadays to be found only in the forests and savannahs of sub-Saharan Africa. Significantly, the animals depicted in the caves did not include camels, which were not introduced into the region until the advent of the Persians in the fifth century BC.

When Almasy explored this area in the early spring of 1933 he found more pictures – and these were of men as well as animals – in caves above Ain Doua, at the level of an ancient lake shoreline. The human figures were dark brown with orange hair, in which they sported white feathers. They carried bows and arrows and wore white belts and bracelets on their arms and legs. In another cave Almasy found a portrayal of what his friend Bermann described as 'an interesting pair: a slender man and an enormous lady – evidently Monsieur and Madam, the owners of this cave, who had decorated their home with their portraits'.

Almasy was to describe his cave art discoveries as surpassing any previously known, anywhere in the world, including the cave paintings in Spain and southern France.* When news of these exciting finds reached the international press later that year, the celebrated German ethnologist, Professor Leo Frobenius,† contacted Almasy and asked to be taken to see them. Almasy was only too willing to mount another expedition to be paid for by a wealthy client and that September he returned to Jebel Uweinat accompanied by Frobenius, the professor's assistant Hans Rohtert and Elisabeth Pauli, a draughtswoman engaged by Frobenius to make copies of the paintings.

While these three were busy in the caves at Ain Doua (where Miss Pauli reportedly copied five hundred pictures in two weeks) Almasy motored 55 miles (90 km.) on to a valley named Karkur Talh with Mohammed Sabr, his Sudanese 'Man Friday'. There Almasy and Sabr found twenty-four more caves containing pictures of a colouring and style different to those around Ain Doua. To Almasy they seemed 'almost futuristic, with modern bold lines'.

* The most celebrated of these caves – at Lascaux – was not discovered until 1940.
† Founder of the Frobenius Institute at Frankfurt's Goethe University. He died in 1938.

Some depicted a curious breed of cattle with downward-pointing horns, giving modern-day credibility to a description by Herodotus of cattle belonging to the Garamantes, the angle of whose elongated horns forced them to walk backwards as they grazed.

Next, Almasy drove another 37 miles (60 km.) on to Jebel Arkenu, a 4,600-foot (1,400-m.) mountain, where he made his 'most beautiful' discovery of all. In the largest of two caves in the rock wall, beside a feature that he was to name Wadi Soura (the Valley of the Pictures),★ Almasy found an entire ceiling covered with paintings, some of them in a new colour: yellow ochre. And among these was a line of gracefully fine-limbed, horizontal human figures whose posture left no doubt that they were swimming. These were surely proof that there had once been a river, or even a lake, in the vicinity. When Almasy showed the swimmers later to Frobenius and his two assistants, they 'could not suppress their wonder'.

That, at least, is Almasy's story and it would seem to be the truth. But Professor Frobenius had a different tale to tell on his return to Germany. In a series of lectures, he claimed the discoveries as his own, by implication reducing Almasy's role to that of hired help. Understandably, Almasy was bitterly angry. In his subsequent account of his explorations he could not bring himself even to mention the name of Frobenius, referring to him only as 'the German professor'

★ It was not, strictly speaking, a wadi but a dried-out inlet meandering between a promontory and two detached outliers of the main Gilf plateau. And the cave was not so much a cave as a hollow at the base of the cliff.

and, with heavy sarcasm, as 'the dear professor, who has forgotten that he only joined me to study the results of my explorations'.*

By the time the controversy erupted, in the winter of 1933–4, Almasy was out of touch with Cairo, leading another motorized desert expedition, but in his absence several British, Egyptian and Italian desert explorers who knew him and his work spoke up on his behalf. Though still resentful, Almasy felt vindicated, but the issue was never properly resolved in his lifetime: Frobenius's scholarly reputation was such that many found it hard to believe that he would make a false claim. On the other hand, those with experience of the corrosive backbiting that can occur in even the most elevated academic circles did not find it beyond belief that the 'dear professor' might make a false, or at best exaggerated, claim to boost his reputation. And it may be significant that, although Frobenius lectured, he never published a learned article on the subject.

It was left to Frobenius's assistant, Rohtert, to put the record straight, but not until a year after Almasy's death. It was 'especially fortunate', he wrote in a monograph published in 1952, that the expedition had been led by Almasy, who had conducted them to 'the most beautiful finds of our journey' – the paintings in the caves of Wadi Soura.

Professor Frobenius was not the only academic to claim credit for Almasy's finds. Professor Count Lodovico di Caporiacco, whom Almasy encountered as one of an Italian

---

* By the time he published a German translation of *The Unknown Sahara* in 1939, Almasy had relented sufficiently to mention Frobenius by name.

military mission surveying Jebel Uweinat in the spring of 1933, further clouded the issue by claiming on his return to Italy that it was he who had found the hitherto undiscovered cave pictures. And to muddy the waters still further, Hans Casparius, the photographer commissioned to take pictures of the spring expedition (he had also accompanied Almasy on the expedition to the eastern side of the Gilf Kebir), appeared to suggest in presenting an exhibition of his work in Paris in 1935 that the credit was his. Success does, indeed, have a hundred fathers.

Finally, there are those who argue that if anyone should be allowed at least a share of the credit for Almasy's discoveries in the Valley of the Pictures it is Mohammed Sabr. By Almasy's own account, his faithful assistant and relief driver did sterling work climbing rocks and examining caves in the murderous heat to help reveal the full scope of the Wadi Soura's Stone Age secrets.

Chapter 10

In his obsessive hunt for the 'lost oasis', Almasy had parsed all the legends, translated all the accounts, studied all the maps, analysed all the histories, revisited all the reports of fellow explorers, past and present, and minutely surveyed the terrain from the ground and from the air.

From this mélange of fiction, fact, observation and speculation, it seemed to him that Zerzura might be almost anything the seeker wished it to be – from an ancient ruined city containing hidden treasure, to a group of lush, settled oases adorned with palm groves, to a mere rock spring providing water and grazing after a once-in-a-generation rainfall. The very existence of such a wide range of possibilities no doubt explained Zerzura's perennial allure: it was the desert Shangri-la. As Ralph Bagnold has said:

I prefer to think of Zerzura as something that has never been seen with human eyes, but only as an image conjured up in the Arab mind of something he would like personally to discover; appearing to the townsman . . . as a treasure city he could loot; to the thirsty Bedouin . . . as a shady oasis similar to those he knew . . . But the Bedouin is not given to self-analysis or to disentangling facts from fancy, so we shall never know the truth.

This may explain the psychology behind the legend itself but it fails to explain the enduring fascination the legend held, not so much for the Arabs but for modern-minded Europeans, such as Almasy, Wingate and Bagnold.

By 1935 Almasy had calculated that the search for Zerzura could be narrowed down to three interconnected, tree-lined wadis scoring the plateau of the otherwise barren Gilf Kebir. Two of these – known to the secretive Senussi and the Tibou of Kufra as Wadi Hamra and Wadi Talh – had been visited by Pat Clayton and had failed to produce even a modicum of hard scientific fact to support the legend of Zerzura. Neither Clayton nor Almasy had yet managed to explore the third and most extensive wadi, which an old Tibou named Nyiaki-Nyiaki had called Wadi Abd el Malik.

Subsequently, Almasy was greatly excited when he learned that in Uweinat, among the many refugees who had fled the Italian assault on Kufra in 1931, there lived an old Zuwaiya named . . . Abd el Malik. Intrigued by the eponym, Almasy tracked the man down and found himself in the presence of 'a withered old man [of] unusual intelligence and perfect memory'.

He astonished me by his ability – quite exceptional with Arabs of his kind – to recognise photographs of people and places that he knew . . . He even drew a map . . . which was astonishingly accurate, both in scale and orientation.

The story that Abd el Malik told Almasy went like this:

Kufra Oasis did not always belong to the Arabs. From long ago it was the land of the Tibou, who owned all the places in the desert for ages. When the Arabs and the Senussi came to Kufra the Tibou left the oasis and went to the Tibesti Mountains that lie 15 days' camel march to the south. Later, when the Senussi began to build houses in Kufra the Tibou returned one by one and lived among the Arabs, but they still owned other places which the Arabs did not know. It was the Tibou who informed the Arabs that there were grazing grounds in Uweinat and also pasture and palm trees in Merga. They also knew other valleys with good grazing such as Zerzura, but no Arab knew that place . . .

One day Idris el Senussi [the temporal and spiritual leader of the Senussi] was in hard need of camels to transport olives from Siwa to Saariet el Taj, but there were no camels in Kufra. A Tibou called Mousa Eid Sigenar told him where he could find the camels of the Tibou in a secret valley four days' march southeast from Kufra inside a big mountain.

Idris el Senussi sent Abd el Malik with another Senussi to find it and

after a certain time [they] came to a large valley that lay at our feet and that was full of green trees . . . There we saw the fresh tracks of camels and also of men . . . The ground of the valley was covered with beautiful tall green grass . . . At the foot of a wall of rocks we found a spring with plenty of good water in it.

There were plenty of camels, too, which Abd el Malik and his companion rounded up and rode off, and also 'mountain sheep and foxes and many small birds in the valley', for which reason Abd el Malik believed that the valley had hitherto been called Wadi Zerzura, the valley of the little birds. When he got back to Kufra and presented the camels to Idris, the Grand Senussi was so delighted that he ordained the wadi should henceforth be called Wadi Abd el Malik (which in addition to honouring the discoverer's name also means the 'valley of the king's servant'). Almasy was greatly impressed by the old man's story. His description of the wadi proved on examination to be 'correct in every detail' and there was no reason to doubt his assumption that the wadi was 'the mysterious Wadi Zerzura of old, even though Zerzura was supposed to be a permanent oasis with date palms and ruins in it'.

Almasy wrote up his account to be presented as a paper at the 1936 annual dinner of the Zerzura Club, to be held, as usual, in the convivial surroundings of London's Café Royal.* His paper concluded with the question: 'Is the reality not more convincing than the suppositions and fantasy-bred rumours?'

But Bagnold remained puzzled. While conceding that there could be little doubt that the wadis of the Gilf Kebir were the truth behind the legends, and commending Almasy for his efforts, he wondered how it was that the Arabic name Zerzura occurred in ancient writings – such as the thirteenth-century *Kitab al Kanuz* (The Book of Hidden Pearls) – centuries before the place was known to the Arabic-speaking Senussi. And that the name Wadi Abd el Malik was mentioned by the English Egyptologist and

---

* Almasy was unable to go to London and in his absence Bagnold read the paper for him.

explorer Sir John Gardner Wilkinson (1797–1875) in an 1835 book, long before the birth of Almasy's informant. 'There is here a serious discrepancy,' Bagnold observed.

I shall continue to think that Zerzura is one of the many names given to the many fabulous cities which the mystery of the great North African desert has for ages created in the minds of those to whom it was hardly accessible; and that to identify Zerzura with any one discovery is but to particularize the general.

Ultimately, Almasy seems to have agreed that a physical Zerzura was not to be found, either in the wadis of the Gilf or anywhere else. 'I have found not a single stone tool, nor a single carved or painted picture in the ancient river valleys,' he wrote. '. . . I have found nothing from later periods either. No ruined city, nor treasure, nor the lost army of Cambyses.'

Almasy recalled that his friend and fellow desert explorer Hassanein Bey had once forecast that in his quest he would find 'rock palaces with walls of onyx and opalescent windows', whose inhabitants would wear jewels, gold and silver and the air of whose gardens would be heavy with the scent of roses. In reality, wrote Almasy, there had been no rock palaces. But he consoled himself with the thought that he had 'truly seen the colours of onyx and opal in the golden gleam of the rising sun and the glitter of jewels in the eyes of the humblest nomads'.

It was Bagnold who was to have the final word on all the generations of striving and fantasy, dreams and disappointments, surrounding the idea of an oasis-city lost in the depths of the desert. 'The Last of the Zerzura Legend' was the uncompromising headline over an article he published in the *Geographical Journal* in 1937.

Zerzura, Bagnold wrote, had become a metaphor for something even more elusive and 'as long as any part of the world remains uninhabited Zerzura will be there, still to be discovered'.

As time goes on it will become smaller, more delicate and specialized, but it will still be there. Only when all the difficulties of travel have been surmounted, when men can wander at will for indefinite periods over tracts of land on which life cannot normally exist, will Zerzura begin to decay . . . Perhaps a long time hence, when all the earth's surface has been seen and surveyed, there may be nothing left to find.

Chapter 11

While Almasy had been in Kufra in 1932, a year after the Italian occupation of the oasis, he had told his hosts about the route he had found through a wadi bisecting the southern end of the Gilf Kebir. It was firm and wide enough to allow heavy traffic through to the hard-surfaced plain beyond, Almasy told Major Ottavio Rolle, Kufra's military governor, and even offered to give him a copy of the map he and his British expedition companions were then preparing.

This readiness to feed information to the Italians may have reflected nothing more sinister than a naive desire by Almasy to brag about his prowess as a desert explorer, regardless of the strategic implications of the data he passed on. On the other hand, it may be taken as evidence that Almasy was spying for the Italians. But if that were the case, why did the Italians suspect that, on the contrary, he was snooping for the British?

'It can be taken for granted that he is an agent of the complex English political-military organization in Egypt,' said Signor Roberto Cantalupo, the Italian Minister in Cairo, in a report to the Ministry of External Affairs in Rome. In this dispatch Cantalupo pointedly referred to Almasy as 'Mister', rather than 'Count', indicating consider-able prior investigation into Almasy's personal affairs.

He even cast doubts on Almasy's motive in telling Major Rolle about the pass through the Gilf. 'This is not tourist information,' he wrote, 'but indication of military aims. It shows that the English want . . . to go from Egypt into Italian territory with heavy convoys.'

The somewhat fevered atmosphere of mutual suspicion, verging on paranoia, between the British and the Italians had been fuelled by Mussolini's expansionist challenge to British interests in Egypt, Sudan and the adjacent Horn of Africa. It was a challenge which even led to talk of 'a new Fashoda' – referring to an incident some thirty-five years before which had brought Britain and France to the very brink of war over possession of the Upper Nile region. In March 1934, Mussolini further intensified Anglo-Italian confrontation by declaring himself (risibly, the Arabs thought) to be 'the guardian of Islam' and champion of Arab nationalism.

Nor could Italy's occupation of Kufra and its designs on the region around Jebel Uweinat – the point where the frontiers of Sudan, Libya and French-ruled Chad converged – be considered strategically insignificant. At Kufra, seemingly secure from attack behind the twin barriers of the Sand Sea and the Gilf, the Italians would be able to build up a considerable force with which to attack vital British installations on the Upper Nile, either directly through El Aqaba, as Almasy had named the wadi bisecting the Gilf plateau, or via Uweinat, some 150 miles further south.

From airstrips at either Kufra or Uweinat, for instance, the Italians could send warplanes to bomb the Nile barrage at Aswan, with potentially catastrophic consequences for the cities of the Nile Valley downstream. And as Bill Kennedy Shaw would point out, a land attack was equally feasible:

From Uweinat to Wadi Halfa is a three days' run over excellent going . . . A force of a hundred or two determined men could have attacked and taken Wadi Halfa, wrecked the dockyard and taken the workshops, sunk any river steamers or barges and made a mess of the Egypt–Sudan line of communications.

Heightening the tension, the Italians had established small garrisons at Ain Doua, south of Jebel Uweinat, and at near-by Sarra Well, both within an area known as the Sarra Triangle which, though nominally part of Sudan, was disputed territory. Against this background, the British Foreign Office noted pointedly that following Almasy's expedition with Clayton, Penderel and Clayton-East-Clayton, he was thereafter invariably accompanied exclusively by nationals of potentially hostile states – Italians, Austrians, Hungarians and Germans. Influenced by what Whitehall called Almasy's 'eccentric and somewhat un-pleasant personality', the tone of the messages between the Foreign Ministry and the British High Commission in Cairo conveyed 'a general suspicion towards [Almasy] and his companions' activities'.

In characterizing Almasy as eccentric and unpleasant, the Foreign Office may have been less than fair. Although he was not universally well regarded by the British, Penderel and the two Claytons got on with Almasy well enough, and at close quarters under testing conditions. And Ralph

Bagnold, in a post-war letter, described him as 'likeable and amusing, although definitely a loner and secretive'.

There was official scepticism over Almasy's having offered the opinion to the Governor of Wadi Halfa, Colonel D. L. Purves, that the Italians were 'getting very tired' of the trouble and expense of occupying Ain Doua and Sarra Well without provoking a British reaction. The Italians' motive in holding these outposts, Almasy reportedly suggested, was to prod Britain into negotiations – not just of the boundary between Libya and Sudan but also between British and Italian Somaliland, where Rome hoped to obtain some concessions. 'This is interesting but does not seem to ring true in view of the steady Italian drive southwards in Libya,' minuted one senior official in the Egyptian Department of the Foreign Office.

Following Hitler's rise to power in Germany in 1933, the Egyptian Department found fresh cause for concern. They were especially interested in one of Almasy's new clients, the thirty-six-year-old Baron Hans-Joachin von der Esch★ – 'rather a mystery man', according to a report to the department from Cairo.

Von der Esch had been one of the first German undergraduates to return to Oxford after World War I and had met his Swedish wife there while she was studying English. In conversation, said the report from the British in Cairo, von der Esch and his wife professed little sympathy for the

---

★ He was the nephew of General Kurt von Schleicher, one-time chief of the German general staff and briefly Reichs Chancellor before Hitler came to power in 1933. Hitler had Schleicher and his wife murdered during the notorious Night of the Long Knives in 1934.

Nazis. They seldom went back to Germany, where his father still lived, and they were generally *mal vu* by the German community of Egypt. They also mixed often with the British in Cairo, both military and civilian, and got on very well with them. On the other hand, the report noted, the couple did 'go about a great deal' with the German Minister and Frau von Stohrer and were generally 'in close touch' with the Legation.

What was more, 'no one seems to know quite what von der Esch is doing here and why he chooses to live in Cairo'. He was ostensibly employed by the local branch of a major German manufacturing firm but it had a very competent manager and assistant manager and his connection with the company was 'rather hard to fathom'. The commercial department of the British mission had 'never been able to trace any salesmanship on his part'. And although the British chancery had to admit that 'nothing definitely sinister' had been found about von der Esch, it went on to note that he seemed to have a lot of spare time and spent much of it on expeditions with Almasy in the desert. Kennedy Shaw, for one, had no reservations about the enigmatic baron. 'That von der Esch was a German spy no one doubted,' he would write.

Either as a cover for their espionage activities or out of genuine curiosity, von der Esch and Almasy had a shared interest in solving the mystery of the lost army of Cambyses. From Kharga in April 1935 they went, together with three Sudanese drivers and three vehicles, across the Sand Sea to look for traces of the fifty-thousand-strong legion which, according to Herodotus, had been swallowed up in the desert while marching from Thebes, via Kharga, to subdue the kingdom of Siwa. 'It is certain,' wrote Herodotus, 'that they neither reached [Siwa] nor ever came back to Egypt.' They had got halfway from Kharga to their objective when, as the Siwans related, 'a wind rose from the south, strong and deadly, bringing with it vast columns of whirling sand which entirely covered up the troops and caused them wholly to disappear'.

Almasy had found an intact Greek amphora at a spot in the Sand Sea between Dakhla Oasis and Siwa and believed it was one of a number cached in advance along the Persian troops' line of march. Now he and von der Esch hoped to find more such significant potsherds which might help them pinpoint the spot at which disaster had overcome the Persians. They were unsuccessful. What they did find was a series of small stone pyramid-shaped markers which Almasy thought might have been guideposts for the lost army.

And at this point they, too, were overtaken by an obliterating sandstorm. It blew without cease for eight days and might easily have cost them their lives. Forced to abandon one car they struck north through the choking *qibli* (sandstorm) in a corridor between the dunes towards Siwa. En route, another car broke down and all five of them had to pile into their one remaining vehicle. It took them another four days to reach Siwa, from which it was relatively easy going to Mersa Matruh on the coast and from there to Alexandria and Cairo.

Had this expedition been a genuine search for the 'lost army' or was it, as some later suspected, a reconnaissance to look for water sources along a potential line of advance from Libya into Egypt? If the latter, the Italians on the spot do not seem to have been let in on the secret. Despite the useful propaganda role Almasy had, intentionally or otherwise, played on their behalf, they remained stubbornly suspicious of him and particularly of a request that he made for permission to use Kufra as a base for an aerial survey of the western side of the Gilf.

His old friend and client, Prince Ferdinand of Lichtenstein, was to be his partner in this enterprise. Lichtenstein had an aircraft equipped with the latest in radio transmitters and receivers and navigational aids and proposed to fly to Libya in the company of a well-known Austrian World War I fighter ace. He wrote to the Italian Minister of Colonies, General Emilio de Bono, stressing how much Almasy appreciated the hospitality he had received at Kufra in 1932 and how useful the cartographic information to be garnered from his planned aerial survey work would be to the Italians.

De Bono referred Lichtenstein's request to Ambassador Roberto Cantalupo in Tripoli and received a negative response. Cantalupo said he believed the British were behind the proposed expedition, noting pointedly that Almasy had been accompanied on his last expedition by three Englishmen and claiming that Almasy's late sponsor, Prince Kemal ed Din, had collaborated with the British. All this coincided with the flare-up of the Italo-British border dispute over the undemarcated territory around Uweinat and the Sarra Triangle. Almasy's proposal was turned down.

Later in 1934 an Italian survey mission under one Captain Marchesi encountered Almasy and Penderel in disputed territory near Jebel Uweinat. When Almasy explained that he and Penderel were looking for Zerzura, Marchesi dismissed the story as 'eyewash' to cover their real motives. Well aware of Almasy's precarious finances, the Italians also wondered how he managed to cover the expenses of his frequent excursions into the desert.

After the outbreak of World War II, when elements of Ralph Bagnold's Long Range Desert Group and a Free French force from Chad occupied Kufra in February 1941, they found a 'most confidential' Italian document which told a somewhat different tale. This was a report to Graziani in Benghazi in which the intelligence officer at Kufra, Captain Cesare Fabri, said that Almasy had advised him to 'be careful' of British intentions over the disputed territory around Uweinat. Fabri reported that Almasy had promised to collect more information on what the British were up to and to pass on his maps showing the best routes, and the location of wells, between Uweinat and the Nile. 'I had the impression,' wrote Fabri, 'that I was with a gentleman and a good friend of Italy.'

Even more confusingly to anyone trying to follow a thread through this maze of contradictions, Almasy (and Penderel, separately) reported to the Egyptian government – and thus indirectly to the British, too – about the Italian military and scientific reconnaissances around Uweinat. When the acting British high commissioner, Ronald Campbell, relayed this information to the Foreign Office, Whitehall agreed that the Italians were getting 'dangerously near' to occupying Uweinat and the wells of the Sarra Triangle, and that something should be done to stop them.

There was no talk of war at this point: the British made a diplomatic protest, followed by an invitation to the Italians to negotiate a settlement of their frontier dispute. In turn, the Italians protested about an RAF reconnaissance flight to Uweinat and the Sarra Triangle, but having made their point agreed to negotiate.

Meanwhile, the British chiefs of defence staff were warning that it was 'essential to put a check on Italian encroachments', particularly towards the Merga Oasis group, lying southeast of the Gilf Kebir and astride a potential invasion route to the Nile. They also pointed out that although the Jebel Uweinat was of limited strategic value it was 'only some 18 hours from the Nile by motor transport and its occupation by a foreign force is therefore undesirable'.

Anglo-Italian talks to demarcate the boundary between Libya and Sudan opened in Rome in November 1933. They were broken off after a few days by the British delegation, whose leader warned that the dispute presented 'the same type of threat to the Middle Nile as the French did to the Upper Nile at the time of Fashoda'. Negotiations resumed after a brief break, however, and came to a successful end in June 1934 with an agreement giving the Italians the wells at Sarra, astride the track leading north to Kufra, and the spring at Ain Doua, to the west of Uweinat. In return, the British retained all territory south of the 20th parallel and east of the 24th meridian, giving them the Merga Oasis, which lay astride the route east to the Nile and Wadi Halfa.

In the following year Almasy inadvertently, deceptively or carelessly gave the Italians further grounds for believing he was using his desert expeditions as cover for intelligence work on behalf of the British. As Anglo–Italian tension mounted in the build-up to the Italian invasion of Abyssinia, he gave an ill-advised interview to a Budapest newspaper in which he was quoted as implying that in the event of war between Britain and Italy he would 'do his bit' for British intelligence. He may have been misquoted; it would certainly have been a wildly indiscreet admission to make if true. However, Almasy was also known to be on friendly terms with the Grand Senussi, Idris, now in exile in Cairo, and the Italians were equally outraged at this and his reported speculations on the possibility of the British mobilizing the Senussi against Libya's Italian occupiers.

Just as damning, he was heard to claim 'British authority' for his proposed future activities on the Egyptian–Libyan border, particularly in the vicinity of Kufra. Also, he had given Pat Clayton a set of photographs he had taken of the Italians' military installations at Kufra.

Not surprisingly, this accumulation of black marks resulted in May 1935 in the Italian rejection of Almasy's request to use Kufra as the base for a renewed search for Zerzura. Later Rome delivered the *coup de grâce* to his plans by issuing a decree barring him as 'an instrument of the English' from any part of Italian territory in Libya.

Despite all this, the British remained suspicious of Almasy. When he and Prince Ferdinand applied in November 1935 for permission to travel overland from Cairo to shoot game in southern Sudan the request was opposed – not by the British missions in Cairo and Khartoum but, as a secret telegram from Sir Miles Lampson reveals, by the

War Office and the Air Ministry in London. 'Military and air authorities are strongly opposed to expedition from Cairo to El Fasher through Western Desert, Oweinat and Northern Province [of Sudan] at present time,' he cabled, 'particularly as party is to be accompanied by Count Almasy who has friends on both sides of the Libyan frontier. They urge therefore that it be arranged that they should travel [by sea] via Port Sudan.'

For his part, the governor-general of Sudan, Sir Stewart Symes, added the caveat that if Almasy's party were to enter via Port Sudan they could do so only on condition that 'cars with light air-wheels are used and the trip is undertaken in winter, without ladies and under an expert guide'.

At this point the British at the highest level were becoming increasingly nervous about the activity of the Germans as well as the Italians. Rome and Berlin were seeking overflight and landing rights from the Egyptian government and mining rights for iron ore at Aswan. 'Sooner or later,' warned London's ambassador to Berlin, Sir Neville Henderson, '. . . the Italians may make an effort to improve their communications with Abyssinia. This would mean war with Britain.' At the same time, Henderson pointed out, 'Germans of all classes are showing increasing interest in the Near East, particularly Egypt'.

In 1936 Mussolini and Hitler joined forces to intervene on the rebel side in the Spanish Civil War, solidifying their relationship further in 1937 by co-signing the Anti-Comintern Pact which formalized, as they put it, 'an axis around which all the European states can assemble'. British intelligence in Egypt went on high alert. Already uneasy about von der Esch, they now turned their attentions to a string of other German 'tourists'.

One British agent went through the luggage of Herr H. W. von Goerschen, who was visiting Sudan, and found a diary containing, *inter alia*, the following passage: 'When the Aswan Dam is closed during the winter months, the quantity of water stored between Aswan and Wadi Halfa is immense . . . Should the Aswan Dam be damaged by dynamite or some other explosive this would be a disaster for Egypt.' No less indiscreet, Lothar Kessler, another German 'tourist' who the British Embassy believed might be an officer in the German Army, 'enquired how many British regiments were stationed in Khartoum and the composition of the RAF squadron [there]'.

By this time Hungary, too, had signed the Anti-Comintern Pact, making it a junior partner in the Axis coalition. And while there is no record of Almasy having been put under surveillance as a consequence, this linkage was scarcely conducive to his hopes of persuading the Egyptian court to nominate him as director of the long-proposed but long-delayed Cairo Desert Institute.

In the spring of 1936, his purported uncle, Bishop Mikes of Szombatheley, asked the Hungarian consul-general in Alexandria to obtain an audience for Almasy with King Fuad to discuss the project. With the help of Fuad's Grand Chamberlain, Zulfikar Pasha, Almasy was granted a half-hour audience with the monarch at which he systematically laid out his detailed proposals. Fuad listened apparently sympathetically and said he would deliver his verdict in due course. About ten days later, the answer came – somewhat peremptorily: the king was not interested.

According to Elizabeth Salett,* the Hungarian consul-general's daughter, in an article written fifty years after the event, Almasy was furious and mistakenly held her father responsible. She said that unknown to her father Fuad had referred Almasy's proposal to Egyptian intelligence and the British High Commission, both of whom had advised against it on the grounds that Almasy's real purpose was to use the Desert Institute as a cover for intelligence activities on behalf of the Axis. 'In 1936,' wrote Mrs Salett, 'it was already known that the Germans were surveying the desert and planning the occupation of Egypt.'

In fact, the Germans had no such intentions at that stage. They regarded North Africa as their Italian ally's bailiwick and it was not until the Italians were heavily defeated by a small British force in early 1941 that they intervened to pull Mussolini's chestnuts out of the fire. And British Foreign Office files contain no mention of Almasy's approaches to King Fuad or of the British response to them – if indeed Britain's advice was ever sought on the matter by the basically pro-German Egyptian court.

---

* Mrs Salett, now a US citizen, is president of the National Multi-Cultural Institute in Washington, DC.

Chapter 12

Barred from Italian territory and somewhat deflated after his search for Zerzura had come to a less than sensational conclusion, Almasy remained in Egypt and redirected his attentions towards his earlier passions – aviation and motor car racing.

He became a founder member of Egypt's Royal Aero Club and a flight instructor at Cairo's Almaza airport,* occasionally returning to his native Hungary to renew social contacts, obtain medical attention for his recurring desert-induced ailments and drum up business.

One successful business venture was to secure the agency of a Hungarian firm that was designing and building gliders. Almasy had one of them shipped to Cairo and flew it around the Pyramids at Giza, a feat that impressed smart Cairenes and helped him clinch a contract for the sale of a number of Hungarian gliders to the aero club. Not that the stunt was really necessary to secure sales and earn him commissions: Almasy was a close friend of the influential Taher Pasha, a nephew of King Fuad and vice-chairman of Misrair, the Egyptian domestic airline. The dandified, monocled Taher

* The close similarity between 'Almaza' and 'Almasy' has led some recent writers on the subject to assert – quite incorrectly – that the airport was named eponymously. The similarity in names is purely coincidental.

was also president of the aero club and its associated gliding school and, more than a friend, Almasy was a semi-permanent house guest at Taher's palatial mansion and his personal pilot. Like Almasy, Taher was a bachelor.

During this period Almasy supplemented his income from aviation and satisfied his longing for wild places by leading small parties of wealthy Hungarians and other European sportsmen on hunting safaris into Sudan, where in the Wadi Hawar there were various species of game. One of these was the addax, the bones of which species Pat Clayton and his companions had found in the Desert Survey expedition to the Sand Sea. Because of its impressive, curved antlers, Almasy was particularly keen to bag a couple of addax for his clients' trophy rooms.

While dining with a group of fellow Europeans at El Fasher one night, he became voluble on the subject. Seizing a scrap of paper he drew sketches of addax and oryx, inspiring Michael Mason, one of the party, to do some sketching of his own.

'Almasy's keen and rather bird-like face invited itself to be caricatured,' he would recall.

So I drew an awful thing of Almasy pursuing an addax at the double. I have often got myself disliked for caricaturing people . . . But Almasy took it in very good part, only insisting that I put as many drops of perspiration falling from the face of the addax as from his own.

With the search for Zerzura no longer preoccupying him, Almasy turned his mind during the mid 1930s to the origins of the Nile Valley's five-thousand-year-old

Pharaonic civilization. Could ancient Egypt's remarkable cultural and technical achievements – the Pyramids, the lavish temples, the sculptures and murals, the icons of sun, snake and ancestor-worship, the hydraulic technology and the intensive agriculture – have originated with the Stone Age people of the Libyan Desert? Almasy believed that while they were herding their flocks and decorating their cave dwellings, the Nile Valley may have been uninhabited: 'It may be assumed that in the rainy period the Nile Valley was unhealthy and it was today's desert that offered favourable living conditions.'

[Their] engravings and later the paintings depicting their every-day life, entertainment and fights attest to their emerging culture. It seems that this settlement pattern did not last long, and the desertification of Libya happened in an intense and relatively short period. The inhabitants first became nomads then were forced to migrate until finally they found a secure living along the now dried-out swamps along the retreating banks of the Nile.

On this assumption, Almasy theorized, Libya could have been the cradle of the ancient Egyptian civilization. 'At least, the discoveries up to now seem to point in this direction, but we are far from drawing firm conclusions . . .' Almasy called for more detailed research to support his theory – and that proved to be its undoing: by the 1970s further research had established beyond reasonable doubt that the origins of Egypt's ancient civilization were indigenous.

Another of Almasy's theories – though of less significance – was that certain Nile-side villages near Wadi Halfa were inhabited by the descendants of Hungarian settlers. Under the Ottoman Empire, five hundred years earlier, they had been brought to the region as janissaries – press-ganged Christian youths from Turkey's Central European and Balkan possessions – to patrol the border. This notion may have seemed plausible, for the villagers in question were noticeably lighter skinned than their surrounding neighbours. But there was no other physical or cultural evidence to support Almany's hypothesis and the origin of these supposed Egypto-Magyars must remain, like Almasy himself, something of an enigma.

While Almasy theorized, his relationship with Taher Pasha was reawakening long-simmering British suspicions. Taher was openly pro-German and dangerously so, in the opinion of Sir Miles Lampson, the British high commissioner – soon to be redesignated ambassador under the 1936 treaty giving Egypt nominal independence. He had 'never liked the man', judging him to be 'very much above himself' and 'violently anti-British'.

But if the British were uneasy about Almasy's connections to the likes of Taher and von der Esch, they might surely have had greater cause for concern over his elder brother's close friendship with Unity Mitford, a fanatically pro-Nazi British society belle whose direct line to the very top of the Nazi hierarchy was to become a matter of public scandal.

The Hon. Unity Mitford, fourth daughter of the eccentric Baron Redesdale and his wife Sydney, was surely predestined to become a Nazi of the deepest dye. She was conceived during a visit by her parents to a small Canadian town in northern Ontario improbably named Swastika (and still so named, despite its evil associations), where Redesdale had extensive mining interests. As if to drive the point home, they had the child – their fifth of seven (six girls and one boy) – baptized Unity Valkyrie. This was an appellation all the more prophetic in that Unity's birth in 1914 long preceded the rise of Hitler and the Nazi Party and the time when Wagner's music became a cultural *leitmotif* of the Nazi regime.

At the age of twenty, and already an ardent black-shirted member of the British Union of Fascists, headed by her sister Diana's lover, Sir Oswald Mosley, Unity was sent by her parents to Munich to learn German at an academy run by one Baroness Laroche. Learning from her tutor that her idol Hitler frequently lunched at the Osteria Bavaria, Unity took to going there in the hope of catching a glimpse of him.

One day in June 1934 she was rewarded when the Fuehrer came in with his bodyguard and a group of hench-men and sat at a nearby table. Unity was so excited that a friend noticed her hand trembling so violently that she could scarcely hold her coffee cup. Three weeks later came the Night of the Long Knives, in which Hitler had many of his old comrades murdered. Much of Germany was shocked by the butchery, but not Unity. 'I am terribly sorry for the Fuehrer,' she wrote to a friend, '. . . it must have been so dreadful for him.'

In the next few months, Unity caught sight of her hero several times at both the Osteria Bavaria and another favourite haunt, the Carlton Tea Rooms. He began to notice her, occasionally nodding as he passed her table, until on 9 February 1935 – 'the most wonderful and beautiful day of my life', she would say – he asked the proprietor of the Osteria who she was and sent him to invite her to join his party.

He doubtless came to regard her – as the daughter of an English peer, and incidentally a distant cousin of Winston Churchill – as a person of potential influence in Britain. But it was clearly her persistence, her blooming (if a little beefy) Nordic good looks and her intense blue eyes that engaged and held the attention of the Nazi leader. Unity's diary reveals that between June 1935 and September 1939, despite recurring international crises that persistently demanded Hitler's attention, they met *tête-à-tête* no fewer than 140 times. It was a relationship of messiah and disciple: there was no hint of a physical nexus. To the worshipful Unity the very idea would have been sacrilege; to the Fuehrer it would have been unthinkable.

It was in 1936 that Laszlo Almasy's brother Janos inserted himself into this unsavoury *pas de deux*. He had become friendly with Unity's older brother Tom, playing host to him at Burg Bernstein, and was close to being Unity's equal in his admiration for the Fuehrer. It was thus only natural that he should extend an invitation to her to visit the castle, whose foreboding medieval atmosphere accorded entirely with her reverence for an unsullied Aryan past.

Equally appealing to Unity was Janos's funereal sense of humour. In the dark, heavily curtained knights' hall adjoining the dining room he had carved the word 'Dracula' on the lintel of the open fireplace and on the desk in his study he had positioned a skull wearing a Jewish *yarmulke*. Less blatantly perhaps, his admiration for the ideology Hitler represented was expressed in the motto he had composed for himself and displayed on Burg Bernstein's grand staircase: 'In life there is no luck, only humanity and order.'

Janos's wife, the pious Princess Maria Rosa, made her own contribution to the dark ambience of Burg Bernstein. In showcases and on the walls and in bookshelves, her collection of holy relics, prayer beads, missals and gruesome depictions of saintly martyrdoms vied for attention with the horoscopes, pentacles and other necromantic arcana that had seemingly obsessed Janos and his father and grandfather, if not Laszlo himself.

After four or five absorbing days as Janos and Maria's house guest, Unity was driven by Janos to Vienna where she caught a train back to Munich. There, better than a thank-you letter, she used her influence to get him an invitation to the next *Parteitag*, the annual Nazi Party rally, with its mind-numbing display of torches, banners, boots, flags and brute triumphalism. Thenceforward Unity and Janos were to become constant companions, travelling together to Berlin for the 1936 Olympic Games, to Bayreuth for the Wagner Festival, to Nuremberg for another *Parteitag*, and so forth. There was scarcely a big Nazi Party occasion at which Janos was not her escort, however discreet.

One event to which even Janos was not invited as Unity's escort was the clandestine wedding in Berlin of her sister Diana to the British Union of Fascists' leader, Sir Oswald Mosley, with Hitler and his propaganda chief, Josef

Goebbels, as witnesses. Diana was as fanatically pro-Nazi as Unity. As British intelligence reports – made public as recently as November 2003 – have revealed, she visited Germany at least fifteen times in 1937 and 1938, bringing back Nazi funds for her husband's movement. Another of the Mitford sisters, the author Nancy, considered Diana's behaviour to be treasonable. She was 'ruthless and shrewd', said Nancy, and 'sincerely desires the downfall of England and democracy generally'.*

Outwardly at least, Janos's crippled wife Maria was complaisant about his relationship with Unity, which may or may not have been physical. 'Unity was not much in love with Janos,' Princess Ina Auersperg told the author David Pryce-Jones, 'Hitler was her one god.' But the Mitford sisters thought otherwise, being 'fairly sure she had a brief love affair with [Janos]'.

On at least one visit together to Budapest, where they stayed at the Almasys' grand family mansion at 29 Miklos Horthy Avenue,† she met Laszlo, home from Egypt to recover from one of the nameless ailments he was constantly picking up in the desert. He occupied a ground-floor flat in the four-storey building which, although the property by inheritance of Princess Maria, was known locally as 'The Almasy House'. That night Unity and the two brothers dined at the fashionable Kis Royale before going on to listen to a gipsy band at the Café Ostende and to dance at the Arizona Bar.

* After the outbreak of war Diana was interned with her husband until 1943 when they were released on grounds of ill health.
† Since renamed Bela Bartok ut.

Among the fashionable crowd they mixed with that night and subsequently was Hannah Mikes, niece of Laszlo's 'uncle', the Bishop of Szombatheley. Unity was introduced to him when she and Janos drove back to Bernstein via Szombatheley after their week in Budapest. She was unfavourably impressed by the good prelate: in the grip of her anti-semitic obsession, she took him for 'a camouflaged Jew'.

Some years later, Hannah Mikes (by then Mrs Van Horne and living in New York) surmised that the cause of Unity's suspicion must have been the fact that her Swiss great-grandfather's name had been Moser – a name that is some-times, though not invariably, considered in Hungary to denote Jewish descent. 'I disliked Unity strongly,' said Mrs Van Horne. 'We called her the Danish cow because she was big, strong and stupid.'

Unity's stupidity combined with her racist obsession inspired her to write a letter for publication to *Der Sturmer*, Nazi Germany's most rabid anti-semitic daily: 'The English have no notion of the Jewish danger . . . England for the English! Out with the Jews!'

She thought it a great joke when she heard how Julius Streicher, proprietor of *Der Sturmer*, had ordered a group of elderly Jews to get on their knees and crop his lawn with their teeth. She accepted and lived with good conscience in a flat that she knew had been confiscated from a Jewish couple in the Schwabing district of Munich; Janos spent five weeks with her in the flat in the summer of 1939, helping her to furnish and redecorate it. And she recounted without shame how she deliberately sent a distressed old

Jewish woman in the wrong direction when she asked the way to the central railway station.

As Nazi Germany absorbed Austria without firing a shot in the 1938 Anschluss, moved on to threaten its next victim, Czechoslovakia, and war loomed closer, Unity conceived it her mission in life to prevent Britain and Germany coming to blows. Throughout the so-called Munich crisis, in which Britain and France allowed the Nazis to dismember Czechoslovakia, Hitler found time for frequent meetings with Unity. Only in the fateful three last weeks of August 1939 were they out of contact with each other, Hitler being otherwise occupied.

On 1 September the Germans invaded Poland; two days later Britain and France declared war. The day after that Unity left her ill-gotten apartment to call on the Gauleiter of Munich, who received her with the respect due to Hitler's most celebrated British admirer. She handed him a sealed letter addressed to the Fuehrer and a similarly sealed envelope containing a suicide note, in which she asked to be buried with her party card and her autographed photograph of Hitler. Then she drove to the Englischer Garten, a noted local beauty spot, sat down on a park bench, drew her pearl-handled Walther 6.35 mm. pistol from her reticule and shot herself in the head.

There is no way of knowing what Laszlo thought of his brother's liaison with Unity Mitford or whether he felt uneasy about the proximity, if even at one remove, that this gave him to the Nazi leadership. Whatever documentary evidence there may be in the form of letters or diary entries is either inaccessible or has not survived. But the link through

Janos with so notoriously public a figure as Unity Mitford must surely have become known to British intelligence. And that intelligence must surely have got back to Cairo.

This makes all the more intriguing an anecdotal report – once again there is no documentary evidence to underpin it – that in the summer of 1939, with the world on the brink of war, Laszlo should have approached the British chief of the Cairo police, Sir Thomas ('Russell Pasha') Russell, volunteering his services as desert adviser to the British armed forces in Egypt.

This may be taken either as a breathtaking display of bluff and bravado by a Nazi agent or as a desperate attempt by a driven but innocent man to avoid being forced by circumstance to leave Egypt and the desert he loved. In the event, Almasy's proposal – if indeed it was made – was turned down and he was told that, as a citizen of a country on close terms with Nazi Germany,[*] he would be well advised to get out or risk internment for the duration of the war that now seemed inevitable.

There is no record of his actual departure from Cairo, but his pilot's licence shows that he made his last flight from Almaza on 22 July 1939, just over a month before Hitler started World War II by invading Poland.

While Janos was involved with the fanatical Unity Mitford during the mid to late 1930s, Laszlo had been conducting an on–off affair with a handsome young actor named Hans

[*] Budapest and Berlin were not yet formerly allied – that was to happen two years further on – but Horthy's Hungary was already Germany's increasingly compliant partner.

Entholt. It is the first and only sexual relationship between Almasy and another man of which we have textual evidence, although unsubstantiated rumours exist of his purportedly predatory sex life in the darker corners of Cairo.

Documentary evidence of Almasy's affair with Entholt resides in a bundle of letters that were discovered at Burg Bernstein in 1995 by the Viennese documentary film-maker Kurt Mayer, whose father Rudi had filmed Almasy's 1929 East African expedition.*

At the outset there is a touchingly naive tone to Entholt's letters, rather like that of a smitten schoolboy: 'I try to let my imagination take me to where you are now. I'd like to drive your car around at the airfield. It would be nice . . .' Almasy was evidently back in Cairo when he received this letter. The following was no doubt sent to him at Castle Bernstein, evidently after the 1938 Anschluss that united Austria with Germany to the huge acclaim of the Viennese.

I am now sitting here again, staring at the wall map. It's a map of Germany and I recently pasted German Austria on it. The line is barely noticeable and I can find my way from here to Vienna without crossing a border to make a guess as to where Bernstein could be.

* In 2003, when the author was researching for this book, he was denied access to those letters and other relevant documents. However, Kurt Mayer had taken extensive notes from this one-sided correspondence for use in a TV documentary and gave the author permission to make use of his translations. The letters lack dates and datelines, but provide a fascinating insight into Almasy's otherwise opaque emotional life.

Obviously, Almasy had not taken Entholt home to meet the family.

As World War II approached the tone of Entholt's letters becomes apprehensive and rather more mature.

My induction into the army is approaching. I am no longer afraid. When the time comes I will leave the past years behind and go in as people probably do when they go into a monastery. Deep inside it will be the same for me. The way everything is blotted out is the same in both cases and only your soul remains; and if you don't have one – machine!

I know your situation very well. I told you long ago that all your adventures were only an escape. How to help you? It's all so difficult when you can't be together with the person you are living for. Loving and longing – it seems that this is the motto of our lives, Laszlo. If it were not for our love one might die of disgust . . .

A later letter reveals that Almasy and Entholt had been discussing politics, a subject on which they seem to have had some disagreement. Acquaintances have suggested that while not in sympathy with Nazi racial ideas Almasy felt there was merit in Hitler's economic and social policies.

What are the differences in the way we see the world [Entholt wrote]? You know I'm not your enemy. Though I'm not against National Socialism I've never had enough clarity to think about it in detail and I've never felt the need. I'm just not politically inclined.

And then there was a rift, obviously not over politics but

---

deeper than a mere lovers' tiff and seemingly caused by Almasy's faithlessness.

You always said that I would be the one to find someone younger and more attractive and you would then have to do without, that you cannot love my love for another. Now, Laszlo, it seems to me that things have turned out somewhat differently and it's up to me to love your love for another. Just go your own way. You will eventually return.

It was an accurate prediction.

Chapter 13

Unity Mitford's suicide bid was a failure. The small-calibre bullet entered her brain but did no fatal damage. A woman out walking in the park with her two sons heard the shot and saw Unity slip from the bench to the ground. One of her sons dragged Unity from the path to lay her on the grass, blood streaming down her face, while his mother ran to a nearby military establishment for help. She had no idea who Unity was. A Luftwaffe car rushed the would-be suicide to hospital and, when they discovered her identity, the police warned the family who had found her not to talk about the incident. It was declared a state secret.

One who was let in on the secret was Janos Almasy; he went into a state of near-panic over the possible consequences to himself of this drama. From Bernstein he contacted Laszlo, by this time back in Hungary, asking him to write to the Redesdales from neutral Budapest, informing them only that Unity was ill and in hospital. They received the letter on 2 October and another came a week or two later, also from Laszlo, saying that Unity was making good progress, but still offering no explanation of her condition.

Meanwhile, a procession of top Nazis, including Goebbels, Ribbentrop and Hitler himself, had been to visit the still-unconscious Unity in Room 22 of the private clinic on

Nussbaumstrasse, where she was under the care of one
of Germany's leading brain surgeons, Professor Heinz
Magnus. He had decided not to try to remove the 6.35-mm.
bullet lodged at the back of her skull. To make the attempt
could prove fatal, he believed.

Her private ward was filled with flowers, among them a
huge bouquet of roses from the Fuehrer, who had interrupted his supervision of the *Blitzkrieg* against Poland to visit
her on 10 September, when he also arranged to pay all her
hospital bills. Three days later she had recovered sufficiently
to exchange a few words with Hitler on the telephone and
on 8 November he visited her again.

He was 'deeply shaken' by her appearance and manner, she apparently having no recollection of her suicide
attempt. Asked what she would like to do, she managed to
mutter that she wished to return to England for a while and
then come back to Munich. When she was deemed fit to
travel, Hitler arranged for her to be taken by special train
to neutral Switzerland where her family could meet her,
take her to France and thence across the Channel to
England.

It was shortly before Christmas that Janos phoned the
Redesdales to tell them that she was coming home. He
took her on to the ambulance train at Munich, accompanied
by a doctor and a nursing nun, and travelled with her as far
as Berne to await the arrival of her parents. They reached
Berne on 29 December and left with her for home, via
Calais, on New Year's Eve.

Unity clung to life until 1948, brain-damaged and incon-
tinent but lovingly attended by her family. Then the bullet

moved and, as Professor Magnus had predicted, she died. It was a kinder fate than that of the millions of victims of the man she so revered.

Laszlo Almasy, by now a reserve lieutenant and flight instructor with the Royal Hungarian Air Force, had not been home in Hungary long before he came to the attention of the Abwehr, German military intelligence, through his book *The Unknown Sahara* which had been published in German translation in 1939.

Although at this point the Germans considered North Africa to be primarily the concern of their Italian ally, Major Franz Seubert, head of the Abwehr's North African desk at the agency's headquarters in Hamburg, was recruiting a staff of orientalists, specialist physicians and others, including the exiled Grand Mufti of Jerusalem, Amin al Husseini, to advise on regional affairs. Accordingly, Seubert suggested to his Balkan-desk colleague, Major Nikolaus Ritter, that he call on Almasy on his next visit to Budapest, friendly to Nazi Germany but still officially neutral in the war that had begun with Hitler's invasion of Poland.

Ritter did as Seubert suggested and was most favourably impressed by Almasy, whom he described as 'a tall, distinguished-looking man, with finely chiselled features . . . a cavalier of the old school'. Over the next few months he spent 'many a pleasant hour in [Almasy's] library, which was overflowing with pictures, souvenirs and weapons from Africa and Arabia'. In the course of one conversation Almasy mentioned that he had been friendly with General Aziz al Masri, an Arab nationalist whom the British had recently eased out of his position as chief of staff of the Egyptian Army.

This gave Ritter 'a fantastic idea . . . it was crazy but it was possible and it made my heart beat faster': what if Almasy might be able to persuade Masri to defect to Germany?

According to Ritter, they began without delay to discuss plans to spirit 'the Pasha', as they called him, from Cairo to Berlin, where he might inspire the younger Egyptian officers, who revered him, to rebel against British domination. 'Almasy was sure that could be done,' Ritter thought. But he was not without reservations concerning Almasy's real motivation: 'His own desire to get back to Egypt might have fostered his conviction.'

In February 1941, after the Germans became actively engaged in the war in North Africa following the British rout of the Italian 10th Army, Ritter's 'fantastic idea' began to take concrete shape. He was appointed to head a *Sonderkommando* (special command) unit charged with getting Masri to Germany, and infiltrating agents into Egypt while, utilizing Almasy's expert knowledge, giving the Afrika Korps the best available advice on desert conditions.

As a first step Almasy was invited to Hamburg, where he discussed maps and equipment for the Ritter Commando with Abwehr officers. Soon after that, by arrangement with the compliant authorities in Budapest, he was seconded from the Hungarian Air Force reserve to the Luftwaffe, given the rank of captain and sent to Tunis as second-in-command of Ritter's special group.

Doctor Istvan Sterbetz, a Hungarian ornithologist, recalled after the war that he and his father had lunch with

Almasy before he left for North Africa. When his father asked Almasy how he could reconcile working for the Germans with his friendship for the British, Almasy replied that he would be doing nothing that was not in accordance with 'military honour'.

Then he stared into space for a long time and slowly added: 'The only thing that really interests me there is to dig out Cambyses! Rommel will supply the petrol . . .' I can still vividly recall the almost crazy, obsessed look on his face . . . I have always felt he would make a pact with the devil himself to further his voyages of discovery: everything else was of secondary importance.

Had Almasy said anything of his politics? 'He didn't reveal any particular political leanings,' said Sterbetz, 'at the most he expressed some unbiased opinions concerning the likely outcome of the war.'

Chapter 14

While Almasy was flirting with German military intelligence, his pre-war desert acquaintances, Bagnold, Clayton, Kennedy Shaw, and a fourth British officer, Captain Rupert Harding-Newman, were setting up and launching the operations of a far more ambitious (and as would transpire far more successful) enterprise than the Ritter Commando – Britain's Long Range Desert Group.

Like so many success stories in British military history, the LRDG was born out of a combination of sheer chance and inspired hunch and sustained by grit, dash and hard-won expertise.

At the outbreak of hostilities Bagnold – still a major, but by then on the retired list – had been recalled to the colours and, as if to demonstrate the War Office's legendary knack for fitting square pegs into round holes, assigned to command a signals unit in Kenya. On the way in convoy through the Mediterranean to East Africa, his ship collided with another vessel and put into Port Said for repairs. Finding himself back in Egypt for a few days, Bagnold decided to look up old friends and caught a train to Cairo.

A brief mention of his return in the *Egyptian Gazette* was brought to the attention of General Sir Archibald Wavell, the British Commander-in-Chief Middle East. Wavell thought, logically enough, that Bagnold would be of more value to the war effort in Egypt than in Kenya and had his posting rescinded. Bagnold was assigned to a Royal Signals unit at Mersa Matruh.

For the first few months of the war, the Middle East remained uneasily quiet while Mussolini dithered over whether to join in the fray alongside his Axis ally. In June 1940, with France about to fall to Hitler's *Blitzkrieg*, he took the plunge and, hyena-like, declared war and seized his neighbour's southeastern flank, the Alpes Maritimes. Further afield, he had long wished to enlarge his North African empire to include Egypt and then by stages to link up, via Sudan, with Somaliland and Abyssinia, his new possessions in the Horn of Africa. His dream was a new Roman imperium of vast dimensions.

Still, it took another three months for him to summon up the nerve to attack the outnumbered British beyond the barbed wire fence that marked Libya's eastern frontier. Finally, on 13 September, his 150,000-strong 10th Army under Marshal Graziani launched the invasion. It was initially successful, driving the British back to Sidi Barrani, fifty miles inside Egypt.

On 9 December the British demonstrated how right Mussolini had been to vacillate. They launched a stunningly successful counter-offensive in which, although fielding only one-fifth as many men as the Italians, they managed in two months to push the enemy back over the frontier and out of Cyrenaica altogether. They took 130,000 prisoners in the process.

Meanwhile, even before the Italians had launched their ill-fated invasion of Egypt, Bagnold had been rethinking his pre-war belief that his travels in the deep desert were just 'for fun' and could never be put to military use. His first proposals for 'a mechanized desert raiding detachment' had been rejected by the commander of British forces in Egypt, General 'Jumbo' Wilson.

Undeterred, Bagnold went over Wilson's head – a risky move for a mere major – and sent Wavell a note asking for an interview. Thanks to an old friend from army college days who was now Wavell's aide-de-camp, Bagnold was facing the C-in-C across his desk within the hour. Boldly, Bagnold produced a copy of his rejected proposal and asked Wavell at least to authorize a small mobile scouting force to find out what the Italians were up to in Kufra and Uweinat. From either or both of those positions, Bagnold suggested, they might be planning to attack the British at Wadi Halfa or further down the Nile at Aswan.

At first, the taciturn Wavell kept his counsel, but when Bagnold added that his patrols might also engage in some acts of 'piracy' the C-in-C permitted himself an unaccustomed smile. He liked that idea, for behind his rather grim exterior Wavell hid an impish streak and was, as Bagnold would say, 'a man of vision and vast knowledge'.

He was also capable of bold snap decisions. There and then he gave Bagnold six weeks to get his patrols organized, equipped and ready for action. And to ensure that his protégé was not hindered by military bureaucracy Wavell dictated an order to heads of departments and branches. Any request Bagnold might make for personnel and equipment should be met 'instantly and without question'. 'What a man!' Bagnold would write. 'In an instant he had given me *carte blanche* to do anything I thought best.' First off, Bagnold sent for Pat Clayton and Bill Kennedy Shaw, the former now a colonial government surveyor in Tanganyika and the latter curator of the Palestine Museum in British-mandated Jerusalem. None of the founding trio was exactly youthful, all having served in World War I. Bagnold was forty-four, Kennedy Shaw was the same age but looked older and Clayton was one year older still, with prematurely white hair.

The fourth but younger founding officer was Rupert Harding-Newman, a fellow member of the Zerzura Club still serving in Egypt (and who at the time of writing is the club's last surviving member, aged ninety-five). His job was to handle the procurement of vehicles and other equipment for the nascent LRDG.

No sooner had they reached Egypt than the two civilians, Clayton and Kennedy Shaw, were commissioned as captains and kitted out accordingly. For his rank and file, Bagnold was given permission to recruit from among the newly arrived New Zealand division. This suited him well: New Zealand farm boys, he felt, would be more adept with machinery and vehicle maintenance than the average town-bred British Tommy.

For transport in the difficult desert terrain, Harding-Newman procured a fleet of thirty new and used 30-cwt. Chevrolet trucks – ten for each of three forty-man patrol units – plus three 15-cwt. command cars. Each patrol was to carry ten Lewis machine-guns, four Boyes anti-tank rifles and one 37-mm. Bofors anti-aircraft gun, plus the Bren light machine-guns, Lee-Enfield rifles and Sten sub-machine-guns carried by all British infantrymen.

Kennedy Shaw taught the young New Zealanders how to use Bagnold's sun compass and other navigational skills, while Bagnold took personal charge of signals training, using Army No. 11 wireless sets which had an official range of only seventy-five miles but which he knew from experience could transmit Morse messages for more than 1,000 miles (1,600 km.) across the desert at certain times of day. The New Zealanders 'took to the strange new life like ducks to water', Bagnold would recall, 'quickly learning the tricky art of driving over dunes, spotting and avoiding the worst kind of dry quicksands'.

Two days before the Italian invaders crossed the frontier, Bagnold and his nascent force set up the first operational LRDG base at Siwa Oasis, sandwiched between the escarpment of the Qattara Depression and the dunes of the Egyptian Sand Sea. They had driven 150 miles (240 km.) across a supposedly impassable dune barrier to get there.

From Siwa, Bagnold sent two patrols to mount a mini counter-invasion of enemy territory. One successfully attacked Italian fuel dumps and emergency landing fields along the Palificata, the signposted, hard-surfaced route to the Italian stronghold at Kufra. The other, commanded by Clayton, passed right through Italian-controlled territory and beyond to make contact with the French forces at Fort Lamy in Chad.

At this point the Chad garrison was undecided whether to join de Gaulle's Free French or remain loyal to the puppet Vichy regime under Marshal Philippe Pétain, who ruled the unoccupied half of France at the Nazis' pleasure. Clayton's unexpected visit was instrumental in encouraging the Chad garrison to throw in their lot with the British.

In contrast to Bagnold's pre-war expeditions, which had all been carried out during the winter months, the LRDG's initial operations were carried out in the paralysing heat of mid September. 'We could not travel at mid-day at all but lay under our trucks and gasped,' Bagnold would recall.

First missions accomplished, the two southern patrols rendezvoused at a pre-positioned supply dump on the southern tip of the Gilf Kebir, from which they motored on together via the Kharga Oasis to Cairo where, linking up with Bagnold, they completed a round trip of four thousand miles, most of it behind enemy lines. Wavell was delighted with his 'mosquito army', promoted Bagnold to lieutenant colonel and gave the go-ahead for three extra patrols to be formed, drawing volunteers from the Brigade of Guards, a Rhodesian regiment and an Indian division.

In December 1940, Bagnold went to Fort Lamy to conclude the negotiations that Clayton had begun. He proved himself as able a diplomat as a desert traveller and Chad came in openly on the Allied side – the only French colony to do so. Soon French troops were in action alongside the newly augmented LRDG in raids led by Clayton – now promoted to major and soon to be awarded the DSO – against Italian positions in the Murzuk Oasis region, six hundred miles west and four hundred miles south of the Italian front line.

From Murzuk they trekked east to join a larger French force from Chad under the command of Colonel Philippe

Leclerc★ in a pending attack on Kufra. Scouting ahead of
the French southwest of Kufra on 29 January, Clayton's T
Patrol was spotted from the air by two enemy planes,
operating in close support of a motorized Italian ground
force, the Auto-Saharan Company. This unit operated in
trucks armed with centrally mounted Breda machine-guns,
giving the appearance from a distance of turreted armoured
cars. Clayton was shepherding his trucks away to safety
when, being the last vehicle of the patrol, he 'got the full
attention' of the circling Italian aircraft.

The neighbouring trucks failed to see that we were hit by the
planes' machine guns. They got me on the head, though the
helmet prevented a wound, and punctured both front tyres and
the radiator. They kept circling and gunning while we changed
both wheels and mounted tyres.

Then Clayton received a bullet wound in his left forearm,
another bullet hit the fuel tank, the engine seized up and
two truckloads of the Auto-Saharans closed in, firing as
they came. There was no alternative but surrender. Clayton
was taken to Kufra, a four-day drive away. There, as he
reported later, 'they were very good to us indeed. Several
of them knew Teddy [Almasy] . . . They fed us with their
own officers.' Clayton was considered a big prize. His
capture was hailed by the official daily *Popolo d'Italia* in
Rome as 'a master-stroke', in which 'the enemy has lost an
irreplaceable element because of his desert experience, and

★ In August 1944, as a major-general, Leclerc led a French division into
newly liberated Paris.

with Clayton some precious documents came into our hands'. From Kufra Clayton was taken to a holding camp in Tripoli and thence to a POW camp in Italy.

In a letter to Clayton's wife, Ellie, following his capture, Bagnold said he was sure the Italians would treat him well – 'letters from other prisoners of war of ours all go to make one believe this'. Of the LRDG raid on Murzuk, preceding Clayton's capture, Bagnold said that 'the whole credit for the great success of that really extraordinary achievement is due to him'. Lieutenant Bruce Ballantyne, second in command of T Patrol, who himself evaded capture and returned safely to Cairo, described Clayton's leadership as 'masterly'.

When the patrol was in action his handling of it was worthy of a professional soldier, which he wasn't . . . He was always leading and showed no personal fear at all. He had one fault, and that was an over readiness to expose himself rather than risk casualties to his men.

Meanwhile Leclerc's force pushed on to Kufra. On the outskirts of Jof they encountered the Auto-Saharans manning a defensive screen. After what was little more than a skirmish the Auto-Saharans took flight and were not to be seen again. Bereft of their only mobile force, the four-hundred-strong garrison shut themselves inside the fort, leaving the French offensive patrols free to roam the oasis at will while Leclerc deployed his mortars and a 75-mm. field gun close enough to fire on the fort through open sights.

From a ruined house near the market place the French

75 mm. lobbed leisurely rounds into the fort until, on 1 March 1941, the defenders ran up the white flag. In the signal room the French found the Italian commander's extravagantly operatic final message: 'We are *in extremis*. Long live Italy. Long live the King-Emperor [Victor Emmanuel II, Italy's nominal head of state]. Long live the Duce. Rome I embrace you.'

Three months later, after Leclerc and the Free French had been redeployed, the LRDG moved its headquarters to Kufra from Siwa, Bagnold becoming in effect military governor of the sprawling oasis complex, almost the size of northern Europe. In deference to de Gaulle's demands – and in recognition of Leclerc's leadership – he flew the tricolour alongside the Union Jack over the fort.

In July 1941, beginning to feel his age, Bagnold was withdrawn from the field to join the intelligence staff in Cairo as a full colonel, not a job he would enjoy. His place as LRDG commander was taken by his recently arrived deputy and former member of the pre-war Zerzura Club, Major Guy Prendergast.

Chapter 15

It was only after the humiliating defeat of Mussolini's 10th Army by the far smaller British* force that Hitler turned his attention, albeit with some urgency, to the North African theatre of war. He had hitherto considered it to be the sole responsibility of his Axis partner, notwithstanding the Abwehr's interest in recruiting a team of Arabists and desert experts such as Almasy.

The strategically vital Suez Canal and the Middle Eastern oilfields seemed not to enter into the Fuehrer's strategic thinking. His mind, and that of his military High Command, the OKW, was already focused on Operation Barbarossa, the planned invasion of Stalin's Russia. So although he designated one of his most dashing field commanders, Lieutenant General Erwin Rommel, to head the hastily formed Afrika Korps, Rommel was given a strictly limited brief. He was to restore Axis prestige by stabilizing the desert front and preventing any further British advance, but no more than that.

Rommel, however, had ideas of his own and, it would seem, a greater grasp of the strategic possibilities of German intervention in the desert than his Fuehrer or his superiors

* In this context the term British should be taken to include the Australian, New Zealand and Indian troops under Wavell's overall command.

at the OKW. From the moment he landed with an advance guard in Tripoli on 12 February 1941 – a mere five days after the Italian mass surrender at a little coastal settlement named Beda Fomm – Rommel began to plan not a blocking operation but a major counter-offensive.

As a sop to Italian pride, he was notionally subordinate to their new commander-in-chief in Libya, General Italo Garibaldi. But by the time the main force of the Afrika Korps – the 5th Light and the 15th Panzer Divisions – began to disembark on 14 February, Rommel and his staff were drawing up the outlines of Operation Sunflower. This was intended to throw the British back beyond the Egyptian frontier, with its ultimate objectives Cairo, Alexandria, the Nile Valley and the Suez Canal.

When Rommel launched Sunflower on 31 March with the Italians in tow, the British were not at all ready for him. Against Wavell's objections their forces had been dangerously depleted by Churchill's decision, for purely political reasons, to counter the German invasion of Greece by sending in the desert army's battle-seasoned Australian 6th Division and the newly arrived New Zealanders, plus a tank brigade. This redeployment reduced British strength to that of a mere frontier force, which might have been enough to deter the demoralized Italians but was scarcely a match for Rommel and his Panzers.

Smashing through a defensive line lightly held by elements of the British 2nd Armoured Division, Rommel's forces took Benghazi within three days. Four days later they captured the British generals Sir Philip Neame and Sir

Richard O'Connor near Derna and by 11 April they were besieging Tobruk (which was to hold out for 242 days until relieved in a British counter-offensive).

Almasy and Ritter arrived in Tripoli a few days before the start of Sunflower with a crew of drivers, wireless operators and other personnel, all members of the crack Brandenburg-Lehr special forces regiment. Officially, Almasy was a citizen of a still-neutral power, which status Hungary retained until – hoping for a share of the spoils – Horthy joined the war alongside Nazi Germany when Hitler attacked Yugoslavia on 6 April 1941.*

The Ritter Commando's brief from the head of the Abwehr, Admiral Wilhelm Canaris,† had been 'to work with but not for' Rommel and his Afrika Korps. In the event, they had no part to play in Operation Sunflower and for the time being they remained in Tripoli, some one thousand miles behind the fast-moving front line. While there, Almasy produced a military–geographical study of the Libyan Desert, based on his personal maps, and gave Rommel's quartermasters expert advice on vehicles, equipment and supplies.

By the time Rommel had run out of fuel for his tanks and Sunflower had consequently run out of steam, the front had stabilized near the Egyptian frontier. There Almasy met the charismatic German commander for the

---

*To his eternal credit, the Hungarian Prime Minister, Pal Teleki, committed suicide in protest.

†In 1944 Canaris was executed for his alleged part in the July bomb plot to assassinate Hitler.

first time and, according to a post-war account of the Abwehr's activities, 'offered to lead a German battalion to Upper Egypt and start a war there, using the Egyptians' hate of the English and love of fascism'. But Rommel did not rise to the bait, if indeed Almasy ever dangled it, because he 'did not have enough officers with experience of the desert. He had no vehicles suitable for the dunes. He also did not have access to the necessary amounts of gasoline . . .'

Was Almasy really so zealous in the service of the Nazi war effort as to suggest fomenting a rebellion in Egypt, or was it all a ploy – as he had confessed to a friend before leaving for North Africa – to extract petrol and vehicles from Rommel in pursuit of his obsessive search for the lost army of Cambyses? We shall probably never know, and it must be mentioned that the history of the Abwehr from which the above quotations come is not entirely accurate on a number of details (including the 'promotion' of Almasy from plain Mister, leap-frogging Count, to Earl).

By the time Ritter and Almasy moved up in the wake of Rommel's advance to set up their operational headquarters at Derna on the Mediterranean, British intelligence had registered their presence in North Africa and was tracking their movements. The British government's ultra-secret Code and Cipher School at Bletchley Park, a Victorian mansion in Buckinghamshire surrounded by gimcrack Nissen huts, had broken the Abwehr's hand cipher and their messages were being monitored by the Radio Security Service. Ritter was 'obviously a man of great importance', reported Captain Hugh Trevor-Roper,* head of the RSS analysis section. 'Ritter, more than anyone else, *is* the Hamburg system.'

Once established at Derna, Ritter and Almasy began to set 'Plan el Masri' in motion, having established contact with the Egyptian general through a clandestine radio link. A portable transmitter had been smuggled into the Hungarian Legation in Cairo via the diplomatic pouch, and from there a wireless operator code-named Martin had been sending enciphered snippets of intelligence and weather reports to the Germans via Budapest.

On the oft-cited Arab principle that 'the enemy of my enemy is my friend', Cairo was a hotbed of pro-Axis sentiment. German and Italian nationals had been deported or interned at the outbreak of war, but there were many others – including Egyptian army officers, politicians and civil servants, bellydancers, musicians and good-time girls, as well as Cairenes employed in the docks and in British supply dumps – who were willing to sell or even give useful information to the Axis. Much of this raw intelligence passed through the Hungarian Legation – and thence to Berlin via Budapest – until the British Embassy persuaded the Egyptian government to withdraw the Hungarians'

---

*Later Regius Professor of Modern History at Oriel College, Oxford, and author of the best-selling *The Last Days of Hitler*. In the 1980s, by then Lord Dacre of Glanton, his reputation was badly tarnished when he certified as authentic a set of fraudulent 'Hitler Diaries' that had been sold by a German con-man to the *Sunday Times* and *Newsweek*.

diplomatic privileges, which meant they could no longer send coded messages.

Undeterred, the Hungarian chargé d'affaires had the Legation's clandestine transmitter removed to the Hungarian church of St Theresa in Shubra where, according to one source, it was hidden under the altar. From there, or elsewhere in the church, the priest in charge, one Father Demetrios, allowed the transmitter to send and receive messages relating to 'Plan el Masri'.

The plan called for Almasy to pilot a Heinkel 111 German light bomber into western Egypt, slipping under the enemy radar screen at the frontier, and to pick up Masri at a prearranged spot, marked by a landing cross on the hard-surfaced *serir* near a prominent landmark known as the Red Jebel.

On the night of 16–17 May Almasy flew to the rendezvous, circling the Red Jebel several times and scanning the desert beyond for sign of Masri. Eventually his fuel ran so low that he had no choice but to return to base, empty-handed and perplexed. What had happened to Masri?

As would be learned later, he and two junior officers had indeed taken off from Cairo on the night in question, with a cover story that they were bound for Baghdad to persuade pro-German Iraqi officers to abandon an anti-British rebellion. In the event, Masri and his companions had travelled little more than ten miles before the engines of their poorly serviced aircraft began to falter and they had to make a forced landing. They managed to return by car to Cairo, where they went into hiding, remaining on the run until 6 June 1941, when they were betrayed and arrested.

This farce was only part of the story. A few days before leaving Cairo, Masri had suggested to a British Special Operations Executive officer, Colonel Cudbert Thornhill, that he be given permission to fly to Baghdad on his proposed mission to stall the officers' revolt. Thornhill would later deny that he had ever agreed to Masri's proposal, but the very fact that he had even discussed it with a character as compromised as Masri was enough to get him sent back to London in disgrace, at the insistence of an irate Ambassador Lampson.

As it happened, the affair was sufficiently embarrassing to the British authorities to save Masri's skin. Rather than endure the inevitable disclosures, they found ways to postpone his trial, on charges which included treason. Court proceedings were put off and put off again and again until they were quietly dropped.

After the failure of 'Plan el Masri' Ritter and Almasy turned to the second task of the Commando – to infiltrate agents into Cairo in an operation code-named Hassan. Despite the Masri fiasco, Ritter was extravagantly optimistic about 'Operation Hassan', reporting to Hamburg: 'Everything in order here. Imminent success in sight.' Again the British were intercepting and deciphering his messages and again the affair was to end in farce. For some reason – apparently because of an absurd mix-up over exactly where 'Hassan' was to rendezvous with his contact in Cairo – the operation was aborted.

Undaunted by repeated failure, Ritter flew to Hamburg to set up the next mission, which was to bring back two spies named Muehlenbruch and Klein, both fluent

Arabic-speakers, for infiltration into Egypt. On 17 June two
Heinkel twin-engined bombers took off from Derna – one
carrying Ritter, the two spies and a motorcycle, the other
flying escort.

As a Hungarian officer on secondment to the Abwehr,
Almasy had the right to decline a mission he felt to be
ill-advised and had refused to be involved. At the last
minute, with the escort plane already airborne, ground staff
engineers had noted something not quite right with the
second Heinkel's undercarriage. Almasy felt that with Lieutenant Guenther Raydt, a pilot lacking desert flying experience, at the controls it would be unacceptably risky to put
the Heinkel down at the proposed landing site. But Ritter
overruled Almasy's demand for the escort plane to be
recalled and the pilots switched. Determined to go ahead
regardless, he stormed aboard the plane with the two agents,
leaving Almasy behind.

Almasy had been right to decline the assignment. When
the two Heinkels reached the spot, some sixty miles beyond
the frontier, where Ritter's plane was to let off the two
agents, leaving them to ride into Cairo on the motorbike,
the pilot baulked. The long shadows thrown by the setting
sun made the makeshift airstrip appear dangerously rocky
and he refused to risk touching down. Ritter, doubtless
bitterly conscious by now that Almasy had been right and
that he should have switched pilots, reluctantly agreed to
return to base, mission unaccomplished.

But as Ritter's plane approached Derna, the town came
under attack by RAF bombers and he was advised urgently
to divert to Benghazi. This was 165 miles further along the

coast and the Heinkel was running low on fuel. Ritter decided they would have to make an emergency landing. But they could find no suitable landing spot until, down to their last few litres of petrol, they radioed for help and ditched in the sea.

In the impact as they hit the surface, Ritter broke his right arm, the pilot broke two ribs, Klein escaped with bruises but Muehlenbruch was crushed to death when a heavy crate broke free from its moorings and fell on him. The survivors drifted in a rubber dinghy for nine hours before they were washed up on the coast between Barce and Derna. After several more hours of pain, exhaustion and raging thirst they were picked up by Storch light air-craft of Rommel's Desert Rescue Service and taken to a field hospital. The escort Heinkel had meanwhile made a successful landing at Benghazi on its last few drops of fuel.

This was Ritter's last hurrah. His arm in a cast, he was flown out to Athens and thence to Germany. It might not be unfair to say that, far from being the top operative Trevor-Roper had taken him for, Ritter was either preter-naturally unlucky or monumentally incompetent. As he would admit in his post-war memoirs: 'I felt that to a great extent I had myself to blame for the failure – initially for not switching planes and then for not having ordered Almasy to take my place. He might have been able to persuade the timid pilot to land.'

Now it was up to Almasy to show that he could do better. Before leaving for Germany, Ritter had passed over command to him. Henceforth the unit was known to the eavesdropping British as the Almasy Commando. And they seem to have had no shortage of quite detailed intelligence about his activities.

On 14 November, Long Range Desert Group headquarters received a message from 8th Army intelligence saying: 'We have reliable information that von Almasy [sic] of Libian [sic] desert fame is about to be given eight [captured] Ford V8s for an unspecified operation employing 2 agents. His part may be to counter your activities.'

Bagnold in Cairo and his LRDG cofounders were surely not surprised to learn that Almasy had turned up in North Africa. As Bill Kennedy Shaw would write in 1945: 'Though the Axis could not produce a counterpart to Bagnold, for Bagnold was unique, they had an *ersatz* Bagnold in Almasy.'

We had realized this as soon as LRDG was formed and kept an eye open for him, for there are ways and means of finding out where people are and what they are doing, even in Hungary in 1940, but in those early days Almasy did not seem likely to give us trouble. A year passed without further news. Then, from a sign here and there, from a letter foolishly preserved by a German soldier,* from a careless word in a prisoner of war cage and from those sources of information which the Censor would strike out if I set them down, we realized that Almasy was on the move.

* Could this have been Entholt?

Chapter 16

The battle for North Africa seesawed. After being driven out of Cyrenaica, the British, under their new C-in-C, General Sir Claude Auchinleck,* launched Operation Crusader, for once catching the canny Rommel unprepared. He was in Rome on holiday with his wife and hurried back post-haste, only to find his forces in some disarray and that Colonel-General Georg von Stumme, whom he had left in command of the Afrika Korps, had died of a heart attack.

In the six weeks of confused and bitter fighting that followed, the British relieved the Tobruk garrison and pushed the Italo-German forces back almost four hundred miles to Mersa el Brega, near the border between Cyrenaica and Tripolitania. In the process, the Almasy Commando had to abandon its base at Derna and head once more back to Tripoli.

Behind his new defensive line at Mersa el Brega, the resilient and ever-resourceful Rommel was very far from defeated. During Christmas and the New Year of 1941–2 he reinforced, resupplied and regrouped and on 21 January launched a new offensive. In turn taking the British by

---

* Churchill had sacked Wavell – unjustly, many thought – after the success of Rommel's counter-offensive.

surprise and racing east again, he recaptured Benghazi and
Derna before coming to a halt on 7 February, on a line
running south into the desert from Gazala, one hundred
miles east along the coastal Via Balbia from Derna. A three-
month lull followed.

Having no direct combat role to play during Rommel's
counter-offensive, Almasy had remained in Tripoli. While
there he drove to the port to pick up some new equipment and fresh personnel arriving from Germany. Among
these was a young man to whom he would refer in his
memoir of the North African war* only as 'the officer
candidate'.

This man was, in fact, Almasy's pre-war lover, Hans
Entholt. Almasy had managed to get him switched to North
Africa from a posting to the Russian front, the pair obviously
having become reconciled since the day Entholt had told
Almasy to 'go your own way'.

At noon [Almasy's memoir ran] I arrive just in time at the
seaplane port. From a distance I recognize the officer candidate
among the passengers approaching on a motor launch. He's an
old friend and I requested his reassignment to my unit. We
haven't seen each other in a long time and my young German
friend has experienced a great deal . . . He has fought in the
Polish and French campaigns; upon learning that I was on the
African front, he badgered me to get him reassigned. Being in
charge of a special detachment, I was entitled to select personally
the members of the unit, but I was reluctant to place a young
man's life at risk under my command.

* *With Rommel's Army in Libya.* See Source Notes and Bibliography.

The risk to his lover's life would have been far greater on the Russian front, of course. 'I just hope we don't have to go farther east,' Enholt had written, 'into that deserted vastness, that solitude stretching farther than the eye can see.' Climate apart, that might as well have been a description of much of the Libyan Desert as of the Russian steppe. But in North Africa Almasy would be on hand to keep a protective eye on his young lover. And before applying for his transfer he had written to Entholt's mother for her opinion.

Her reply, no doubt embellished by Dr Goebbels' minions before they passed Almasy's manuscript for publication, reads like pure Nazi propaganda: 'Regardless of where my son serves, he will be fighting for his homeland . . . I know that my son would fulfil his duty under your command just as he would under any other assignment. His fate and yours are in the hands of Providence.'

On Entholt's arrival in Tripoli, Almasy was glad to find that he '[hadn't] changed at all' since their last meeting. 'I can tell from the expression on his face that he's genuinely happy to see me again. He looks dismayed only upon learning that I need to leave for the front tomorrow morning but will not be able to take him with me. He'll have to wait here in Tripoli until I can arrange for him to rejoin us.' That night Almasy dined out with Entholt and the German consul, Sepp von Walther. At dinner Walther was called away to the phone, returning with a smile to announce that Rommel had taken Benghazi. Anticipating the fall of Derna too, Almasy was already planning to leave the next morning for the front.

He had no room in his car for Entholt but Walther said he intended to drive two days later to Benghazi and offered to give Entholt a lift. Almasy considered the consul to be a reckless driver and half-jokingly demurred: 'I bet that if my young friend is placed under your care, the next time I see him will be in hospital, if he's lucky.' But Entholt was insistent.

My officer candidate pleads with me to let him accompany the consul. We joke . . . that it's not a good thing to be in such a hurry to get to the hospital, but we finally agree that if Allah so wishes we'll meet in Benghazi in four days.

Almasy was to win his wager – not through the consul's driving recklessly but because of constant RAF attacks on traffic along the Via Balbia. On his way to Derna, Almasy had some nasty experiences of those. Driving east, about 450 miles from Tripoli, he noticed a small dark blip on the horizon and drove off the road to shelter behind a sand dune. It was not yet possible to tell if the approaching aircraft was friend or foe, but Almasy was taking no chances. The distant hammering of the plane's machine-guns gave the answer and Almasy yelled to his radio operator to get away from the car.

The plane comes like an arrow from hell, skimming a few metres above the highway. The pilot really knows his business . . . He'll be on us in seconds . . . I can make out his profile for an instant behind the windshield. Suddenly a sub-machine gun is fired right next to me. The radio operator is standing there with legs akimbo, blasting away at the enemy plane . . .

The plane veered off and vanished. It had done a good deal of damage. A few kilometres further along the highway Almasy came across the blaze of a huge Italian truck laden with fuel drums. A column of oily black smoke rose over the desert. Several of the crew were injured or dead. 'This is an ugly business, hunting down vehicles on the highway,' Almasy thought.

On the outskirts of Benghazi, while waiting for permission to acquire some captured enemy vehicles best suited for driving in the deep desert, Almasy was camping for the night when he heard the rumble of approaching enemy bombers and dived into a ditch.

I burrowed into the ground and tried to make my head disappear between my shoulders at the hateful, ghastly whoosh of incoming bombs . . . I knew from experience that . . . if the swishing sound becomes a chirp the bomb will land damned close to our heads, if not right on them.

The attack went on uninterrupted for two hours. Almasy emerged 'cowering and clawing but alive and unhurt' and wondering why the enemy had paid so much attention to an apparently valueless target. He soon found out when 'a new, unfamiliar clamour arose; a diabolic symphony of hissing and popping, large and small detonations and sharp crackling'. He had inadvertently stopped for the night close to an ammunition dump the British had left behind in their retreat. The RAF had come back to destroy it.

The morning after arriving in Benghazi, Almasy was awakened by Walther, standing by his bed in bloodied civilian clothes. 'The doctor says it's not serious,' Walther told him, but the officer candidate (as Almasy continued to call Entholt in his memoir) 'was wounded last night, but only slightly. It really worries me that you won your bet.' Almasy's memoir – so discreet, yet at the same time so revealing – continues:

I can hardly wait until we arrive at the hospital . . . I feel a heavy sense of responsibility. Hurrying through the crowded hospital, I see my friend with his bandaged head at the end of a ward. I'm still not sure how serious his wound is, but the big smile with which he greets me suggests that it can't be very bad. As soon as I arrive next to the bed, the young man's body stiffens to attention under the blanket. 'Captain, I humbly report for duty and ask permission to leave here immediately.'

In the ensuing weeks, as the British code-breakers continued to read the Almasy Commando's wireless traffic, they grew to consider that a rival to their own Long Range Desert Group might be in the making. This impression was strengthened when, in early May 1942, during the lull along the Gazala line, they learned that Almasy was preparing to embark on a major operation code-named Salam. Although for the time being its objectives remained obscure, Salam's purpose was to infiltrate two agents into the Nile Valley, and thence into Cairo, but not this time by air, as previously.

Almasy was to *drive* the agents across the desert, starting from Jalo, a fly-blown oasis on the edge of the Colanscio Sand Sea, astride the Palificata Track between the Mediterranean coast and Kufra. It was to be a hazardous and gruelling journey across enemy-held terrain and one that, on the Axis side, only Almasy had the knowledge and desert experience to achieve.

The Bletchley Park intercepts of the Almasy Commando's wireless traffic were to be belatedly augmented by the contents of a notebook and other papers captured from a detachment of the Brandenburgers in an ambush in the desert near Bir Hacheim on 29 May. These documents contained details about Operation Salam's wireless telegraphy (w/t) and other arrangements that might have been of great intelligence value to the British had they been received in time.

There were to be daily transmissions at 1800 hours, Tripoli time, said a message from 8th Army Intelligence to LRDG headquarters, and the code-names Wido, Salam, Kondor, Schildkrote, Otter and Adolf were noted. All 'out' messages dealing with w/t matters were to be signed 'Schildkrote' (tortoise).

The first day of travel for this operation was given as 12 May and w/t routines were given for the succeeding twenty-four days. Among various 'in' messages the most interesting was one signed 'Sandy', who would turn out to be one of the two infiltrated spies, making clear his intention to stay off the air until they were safely installed in Cairo: 'Leaving midday today. I will not call you up by wireless until I have reached my destination. Wish me all the best of luck.'

Somewhat obscurely, the captured documents also recorded amounts of English money against various items such as soap and bottles of cognac. 'In view of the large sums involved and the smallness of the numbers of bars of soap, etc., it is thought possible that these are code entries,' said the 8th Army intelligence report. Equally obscure were 'detailed instructions for a cipher which is based on an ordinary book, for example it may be a work of fiction or history, but no details as to its nature are given'.

Although these revealing documents did not fall into British hands until Operation Salam had been successfully concluded, Almasy might well have felt uneasy about the enemy's awareness of his movements when he set out from Jalo on 12 May. Not only had the boffins at Bletchley Park cracked the Abwehr hand code: they also had the key to the Germans' supposedly impenetrable Enigma machine, and would thus be able to decrypt the progress reports and other messages Almasy's wireless operator was supposed to send to the receiving station code-named 'Schildkrote'.

Chapter 17

At the age of eighty-five, Jean Howard might have stepped straight from the pages of a John le Carré novel. She has all the characteristics le Carré has taught us to expect of a retired lady spook — a sharply etched world view, a cantankerous wit, a mischievous edge and a near-total recall, all these lurking and ready to pounce from inside the stooped figure of the well-bred beauty she once was.

Mrs Howard lives, surrounded by books and box files, in a comfortable fourth-floor flat above the high-fashion shops at the Knightsbridge end of London's Sloane Street, hard by Harrods and Harvey Nichols. But fashion and high living are the least of her interests. These derive mainly from her World War II service as an analyst and translator at Bletchley Park, nerve centre of Britain's cipher war effort, and her Cold War service (which she denies *pro forma*) with MI6. A lifetime of knowing official secrets — and keeping them — has made her discreet although far from tight-lipped. Simultaneously voluble and Delphic, she talks freely, scatters hints like confetti and gives away little.

At the age of only twenty-four, her service at Bletchley Park made her privy to one of World War II's most closely held secrets — that Britain had cracked Germany's supposedly impenetrable Enigma coding machine, allowing unparalleled access to the enemy's most important tactical and strategic decisions. So crucial was this so-called Ultra Secret that for almost thirty years after the war Mrs Howard and others in an exclusive circle of Bletchley Park cryptologists, analysts and linguists, their immediate bosses, the most senior military and naval officers and need-to-know wartime cabinet ministers, were bound by an oath of silence not to reveal it.

When the British government declassified the Ultra Secret in 1974 a lot of military history had to be rewritten and judgements of wartime strategies – and of individual wartime commanders – had to be revised. But Jean Howard was less concerned with the big picture than with the fine detail concerning a particular enemy agent: Laszlo Almasy. It would be only a slight exaggeration to say that she is obsessed by the man. His life and exploits bridge both phases of her career. But although she never met him in the flesh, over the years she has developed an almost proprietary interest in him.

Almasy's name first came to her attention in the spring of 1942 when, as Miss Jean Alington, a linguist working in Hut Three at Bletchley Park, she noticed some Enigma intercepts relating to an 'Almasy Commando' which had been overlooked by her superiors. At that time the clandestine activities of an obscure Hungarian desert expert attached to the Afrika Korps were not a matter of high priority to her superiors. They were, after all, preoccupied with matters of far greater strategic import, not the least of these – so far as the desert war was concerned – being when Rommel might launch his next offensive. But Jean Alington felt a compelling urge to fine-focus on the information that was intermittently crossing her desk about a forthcoming Almasy Commando operation, code-named Salam.★

'I had noticed that this Almasy Commando was to go through a part of North Africa [somewhere near the Qattara Depression, south of the British defensive line at El Alamein] where we had a false army – a signals unit, not tanks etcetera, but signals being sent out to look as though it was an entire army', she would recall.

So she asked her superiors for permission to search for more relevant Abwehr decodes so that she could keep an especially close watch on Almasy's movements. They gave her the go-ahead, but only grudgingly. 'All right,' they conceded, 'but do it in your own time.'

'I thought "this man must be caught",' she told a 1995 television documentary interviewer.

It would be terrible if we didn't send someone to catch him before he discovered the truth about our phantom army. So I got permission to send a message to Cairo that aircraft should fly from Kufra Oasis to look for him and alternatively that we should send people up from the south to do what they could, but to pick them up alive. It seemed to me very important not to kill them but to pick them up alive.

This precautionary note was necessary not only, as Mrs Howard put it, 'to find out what they were up to', but, above all, to protect the Ultra Secret.

★

★ Which she spotted as an anagram of Almasy without the final letter and thought piquant since *salam* is the Arabic for 'peace'.

Almasy's Operation Salam began on 29 April 1942 with what may be considered a questionable operational decision on his part. With one exception, his seven-man team (not including the two spies they were to inject into the Nile Valley) were highly trained special forces troopers of the Bradenburg-Lehr regiment. The one exception was the 'officer candidate', Hans Entholt.

As commander of a special unit, Almasy was not answerable to a superior officer for his choice of personnel for a particular operation and one can only speculate as to how he rationalized to himself – if rationale entered into it – his reasons for taking Entholt along as medical orderly. Was he really so besotted that he could not bear to be parted from his lover for two or three weeks?

As things transpired, he was to be spared the possible consequences of this decision. Two days out from their starting point at Jalo, Entholt and Almasy's seasoned wireless communications expert, Sergeant-Major Hans von Steffens, were stricken with severe desert colic. As their condition worsened they became disoriented and Almasy decided to turn back to Jalo.

He would have been obliged to do so anyway: he had found his intended route – southeast towards the Qattara Depression – barred by sand dunes that were unmarked on the Italian maps and impassable to his heavily laden vehicles. By the time they got back to Jalo, on 6 May, Entholt and Steffens seemed so ill that Almasy felt obliged to send them both back to Tripoli for emergency treatment. (After they reached Tripoli the German consul Walther sent Almasy a personal signal saying that Entholt was 'not fit to travel but not dangerously ill'. This was followed five days later by another message saying that both Entholt and Steffens had been sent on to a military hospital in Germany.)

With or without them, Operation Salam had to proceed and, after making an aerial survey, Almasy resolved to try a more southerly route, setting out once more on 11 May. But having made camp at a point 170 miles (275 km.) south of Jalo, he was forced to think yet again after calculating belatedly that his five remaining vehicles – three 30-cwt. Bedford trucks and two Ford V8 station wagons, all of them captured from the British* – could not carry enough supplies to get his team through heavy dune country to their destination and back.

So, during the night everything was recalculated once more and the trip reorganized to take a longer but less punishing route. They would proceed down the well-marked, hard-surfaced Palificata to the outskirts of the Kufra Oasis complex, turn east from there to round the Gilf Kebir escarpment and thence east again to Kharga – a route that Almasy knew so well from the old days.

This would be risky since Kufra was in British hands, and it would involve a detour of 310 miles (500 km.) on both the outward and return journeys, making a round trip of 2,600 miles (4,180 km.). But there was no alternative. 'We must go via Kufra!' Almasy wrote in a diary note dated 15 May, 'the task must be carried out.'

The new plan would also mean reducing still further

---

*In the seesawing North African campaign, vehicles of both sides frequently fell undamaged into enemy hands.

the number of his vehicles and personnel: 'Only thus will supplies of fuel and water be adequate.' Accordingly he sent two men back to Jalo in one of the Bedford trucks, leaving him with two Ford V8s and two Bedfords to complete the journey. These all bore the Afrika Korps markings of the 21st Panzer Division with faded German black crosses on their doors, formally complying with the rules of war even though the divisional markings were artfully obscured by layers of desert sand.

Those travelling on with Almasy were to be three Brandenburger corporals – Munz, Woehrmann and Koerper – and the two Cairo-bound agents, Johann Eppler and Heinrich ('Sandy') Sandstette. Eppler was a German-born Egyptian citizen, speaking excellent English and Arabic as well as his native tongue. After his parents' divorce his mother had married a prominent Cairo judge who had formally adopted the boy, giving him the name Hussein Ghaffar.

Sandstette, like Eppler in his late twenties, had spent several years before the war working and travelling around Africa. He too spoke good English, although with a slight American accent, and the Abwehr had provided him with a forged British passport in the name of Peter Muncaster.

Almasy had code-named the two men Pit and Pan, and if the implications of a knockabout comedy duo suggest that they were not to be taken entirely seriously, that does seem to be the case. 'Pit and Pan are not overjoyed at [the prospect of] driving through Kufra,' wrote Almasy as they started out once more. 'They fear an encounter with the enemy.' A few days later into the trek he had cause to comment on their sloppy personal habits: 'Pit and Pan, who are riding in the radio car, are the most untidy fellows I've ever had under me. The inside of the radio car looks frightful – loads, personal effects, weapons and food all mixed up together.'

Almasy did not seem to rate his three remaining Branden-burgers highly, either. '[Woehrmann] has no initiative and I have to keep asking and ordering everything,' he wrote. 'The men still cannot understand, anyway, that despite [my] experience in the sea of sand, a long-range expedition through this realm of death is nothing else than a flight from the desert itself.' But despite his misgivings about the quality of his personnel, Almasy's diary reveals no reservations about the operation itself. It seems that returning to his old stamping grounds and testing his skills against the worst the desert and the enemy had to offer outweighed any consideration of risk or fear of failure.

Almasy's party left Campo 4 at 8.30 a.m. on 15 May and about four hours later they were driving down the Palificata near a British military post at Bir Abu Zereigh, in the north of the extensive Kufra Oasis. 'I drove through it purposely at noon-time,' Almasy wrote, 'that's when Tommy is asleep, too.' Another complaint about his personnel came soon after: 'At 3 o'clock Pan gets hopelessly stuck [in soft sand]. The men work for 2 hours until "Maria" [one of the Bedford trucks] is free.'

Scarcely are we on firm ground when we are lucky: I find the traces of the old Trucchi Track from the years 1932–35. At that time the Palificata did not yet exist and the heavy diesel trucks made a way through the hills with their double tyres. It is easy to keep to the track. We 'lagered up' on it . . . at 1900 hours. Day's performance, 210 km.

At this point, Almasy stashed four cans of petrol and two cans of water for the return journey, concealing them behind a nearby crag. The following day his party crossed 'extremely difficult' terrain, but were thankful for a thick sand cloud which made enemy aerial reconnaissance impossible. Then came a 'big surprise'. Due east of Jof, the main town of the Kufra Oasis, where ten years before he had been feted and toasted by the Italians, Almasy came across the fresh tracks of more than a hundred trucks.

I had no idea that enemy [supply] columns were running from the East towards Kufra . . . So we alter course and follow the tracks eastwards. Duney sand, heavy going. Tommy has also ploughed in deeply and often stuck. Finally I am able to ascertain from a reversing track that half of the big column's tracks are without doubt this morning's, the first ones about 2 days old.

That evening, having again covered 155 miles (250 km.), they made camp in a saddle between two hills and left another cache for the return journey – six cans of petrol, one can of water and one case of rations. Almasy wanted to radio back a report about the British lines of communication, but Woehrmann was unable to contact either 'Otter' or 'Schildkrote'.

The following morning, while trying to pick up his old route between Kufra and the Gilf Kebir, Almasy was irritated to see his way barred by a range of hills that were, again, not shown on his Italian map: 'No mapping was done here outside the Depression and the Jebel Kufra. What were they doing from 1932–39 then?' Turning south to circumvent the hills, Almasy came across hundreds of tracks and two abandoned Bedford trucks, bearing the identification markings of the Sudan Defence Force. He checked the odometer of one, which read 433 miles. 'The puzzle is solved,' he exulted, 'the trucks have come from Wadi Halfa. Thus the assumption hitherto held that Kufra is supplied from the south, from French territory, is not correct. Wadi Halfa . . . is the reinforcement base.'

Further on towards the Gilf, Almasy found the terrain 'horrible'.

Dissected plateaux, soft shifting sand, tail dunes of the 'garas' [sandhills], forever having to change course and check bearings for finding new ways through. Since Woehrmann is not capable of reckoning bearings and distances for me, I am constantly forced to stop and to check the courses on the useless Italian map. [The dunes are] Impassable with the overloaded vehicles, so turn about and go N. to cut across the bit enemy L of C [lines of communication] again. A detour of 100 km. Frightful!

At last Almasy led his vehicles on to a stony plain of black shale where innumerable enemy tracks merged into a veritable road – 'an Autobahn', as his men said. Now the going was much easier, but with so many British in the vicinity 'caution [was] imperative'. And, indeed, before long Almasy spotted clouds of dust ahead. He turned off and led his little column into concealment behind a small group of rocks. Through his binoculars he could see five dust plumes: 'We must drive carefully in order not to overtake the Tommy column inadvertently.' But through his glasses Almasy had spotted a more encouraging sight than the enemy: 'Along the E. horizon the majestic rock escarpment of the Gilf Kebir . . . At last I am on familiar territory, and after a few km even on my own map. *Allahu Akhbar*.'

After a short time we drive through the only possible way which I found here before, the narrow defile between the two round white juts of rock which I then named 'el Bab el Misr' (the Gateway to Egypt) . . . Now everything is familiar to me . . . [even though] the war has drawn its traces with giant claws in this hidden and secret world.

As soon as possible, Almasy veered off the enemy's tracks, hugging the escarpment and heading towards the southwest spur of the Gilf, and nothing more was seen of the British vehicles' dust plumes. They 'lagered up' at 6.30 p.m. on the 17th and stashed some more supplies – six cans of petrol, three cans of water and a day's rations for four men. They also left behind one of the Bedfords, hiding it deep inside a rock cleft after painting over its identification markings and removing everything that might provide a clue to its mission. On the inside of the windscreen Almasy left a sign, in French, saying: 'This vehicle is not abandoned. It will return to Kufra. Do not remove any part.'

The Tommies are to think the vehicle belongs to their de Gaullist allies. The maps and log books hitherto used are forbidden. If they catch us they can rack their brains as to where we have come from.

The next morning they drove on with three vehicles, having redistributed the loads, and soon they reached Almasy's Wadi Soura, the Valley of the Pictures, where Almasy had found the cave paintings nine years before. For him it was an intensely nostalgic experience. They stopped to take photographs and inside the main cave, where Almasy showed his team the swimmers and other rock paintings, 'one of the men pick[ed] up an India rubber of German make, "Reform". My companion Miss Pauli lost it there at that time, when she was copying the cave pictures.'

Further on, they encountered the triple peaks of the Drei Burgen (Three Castles), where Almasy had established a water store in 1932 and replenished it the following year. Recalling that this cache had saved the lives of Bagnold and a travelling companion in 1935, when one of their vehicles broke down and they were stranded for eight days, Almasy found eight water cans still *in situ*. Some were rusted through, but four still contained water.

I open one cautiously in order not to shake up the water. We pour it into a cooking pot. It is clear and odourless. Each of us takes a sample of the 1933 vintage and we find the water excellent!

In the plain below, once a landing strip for *Rupert*, Almasy spotted a group of parked enemy vehicles. After watching for some time and seeing no movement, he drove down cautiously with Munz, leaving the others behind. He found six unattended 5-ton trucks belonging to the Sudan Defence Force, some laden with empty petrol drums and all refuelled for an intended return journey. Almasy calculated that the trucks' fuel tanks contained some 500 litres of petrol between them and that with this extra fuel he could comfortably reach his objective with the two Ford V8s and even pick up one of the Bedfords on the return journey.

Summoning the rest of his team, Almasy emptied the contents of the fuel tanks into the empty drums and loaded them on to his Bedford. Then he set about sabotaging the 5-tonners: 'They shan't fight against us any more; off with the cap of the oil filter pipe and several handfuls of finest desert sand put in. Very carefully and cleanly so that nothing shall be noticeable.'

That done, Almasy led his convoy 12 miles (20 km.) into foothills to the northeast to cache the looted petrol, distributing the drums 'artistically among the black rocks so that none could be seen, even from vehicles that might follow our tracks'.

As they drove on next day, the 19th, Almasy had difficulty finding the entrance to El Aqaba, the wadi cutting through the Gilf plateau to reach the hard-surfaced plain beyond, which he had discovered ten years before. It was a 'bad day', in which to add to his frustration he broke a spring on his vehicle and clocked up a total of only 50 miles (80 km.). That night there were 'depressed spirits in our camp'.

Next morning there were again 'frightful driving conditions', but this time Almasy found El Aqaba and was delighted to note that only his own tyre tracks from ten years before were visible in the dry river bed: 'The enemy no doubt looked for *Aqaba* but didn't find it,' he exulted. But soon his mood changed. Negotiating a tail-dune lying athwart the exit from El Aqaba to the plain, Almasy again had cause for complaint about the men under his command.

Pit as usual drives like a wild man and instead of following any track he drives 'the President' head over heels down over the steep part of the tail-dune. A miracle that the vehicle does not overturn at the bottom. Result: broken track-rod on the shock absorber. Altogether except for Munz the men cannot drive . . . How different were my Sudanese!★

The next day, 21 May, was

the hardest so far as regards terrain. Low plateaus and over and over again small hills with the tail-dunes which are such a nuisance, broad plains with shale stretches and only now and again a piece of open *serir*. The vehicles suffer terribly on this kind of ground, the drivers behind me as well, probably . . . My eyes ache terribly from eternal compass-driving.

After leaving behind the last remaining Bedford with a cache of water and petrol they camped for the night near a feature called the Zwei Bruste (Two Breasts) on the eastern slope of the Gilf. There they found that radio

★ This remark is in glaring contrast to what Almasy had to say in *With Rommel's Army in Libya*, where he appears to trash his pre-war Sudanese crews in favour of 'these blue-eyed, blond German boys who have only been in Africa a few months, yet they act as though the only life they've ever known is that of a long-range desert scout'. We may safely assume that this phraseology – not Almasy's style at all – was inserted by the Nazi Propaganda Ministry, through whose hands his manuscript must have passed before publication.

communication had broken down again, prompting another diary outburst from Almasy.

Woehrmann reports that the transformer is not working. The men mess around with it for an hour then come in, with the thing still out of action, to our one-pot supper. Three radio operators and a mechanic are not in a position to find out what is wrong! In this undertaking I always have to do absolutely everything myself.

Almasy found the fault in a few minutes – 'the lead-in to the transformer had been snipped through by some angular object'. But when he ordered Woehrmann to lay in a new lead, the corporal said he could not do it, having had no technical training. Furious, Almasy laid the lead himself, but still the transformer did not work. After a new examination by torchlight, he found that the compound lead was out as well.

Now at last the transformer's running, but there's still no contact. Now the fault is supposed to be in the instrument itself! I am not a radio mechanic and I can do no more to help. Tomorrow Pit must try with his instrument.

The next day, 22 May, as they headed east towards the Kharga Oasis, Almasy told his men about the desperate flight of the Kufra refugees in 1931, an event which he now called 'the greatest tragedy of the Libyan Desert'. Just a few kilometres on his story 'met with sad confirmation – a few camels' skeletons, a human skull bleached snow-white and actually the touchingly narrow tracks of the high pressure tyres of the Mamur's [the Dakhla police chief's] two Fords'.

By that evening Pit's transmitter was working perfectly and he sent out his call sign to Schildkrote: 'We watch, holding our breath, thronging around him and listen to the whistling in the headphones. *Schildkrote* does not answer.' Almasy now vented his frustration on Rommel's signals personnel.

I have scarcely enough petrol to get back. Everything was discussed and planned in detail. I was only to radio and they would drop fuel, water and food for me in any grid square I liked. Now the instrument which is tuned to our point of departure has fallen out and the called station on the other does not answer! Probably there's another shift going on there. I begged them to leave *Schildkrote* at one fixed point.

After camping for the night near the western edge of the Kharga Oasis, Almasy set out on the 23rd determined to reach the drop-off point for Pit and Pan – walking distance from the Nile Valley city of Assiut – and to start his return journey before nightfall. To save precious petrol he would risk taking the road to Kharga instead of driving over the dunes.

I know everything here, the scattered *barchana* [crescent dunes] of the *Abu Moharig* dunes, through which the road snakes in a masterly fashion, the iron tracks of the abandoned railway lines . . . on the left hand *Jebel Ter* and on the eastern horizon in the soft red of breaking day the mighty wall of the Egyptian limestone plateau.

Five kilometres from Kharga, Almasy told the men in the following car – Munz, Woehrmann and Pan – to keep up with him under all circumstances, to halt when he halted and start up when he started up, and to have their sub-machine-guns at the ready. 'But arms should not be resorted to unless I myself have started it.'

In the town square they were stopped by two *ghaffirs* (night-watchmen), one of whom carried a pistol. 'One of them gives a respectful greeting in Arabic, points to his mouth and says "no inglizi". I return the greeting and tell them that I speak Arabic.' The watchman told Almasy he had to report to the *Markaz*, the administrative centre. Almasy replied that he was merely carrying the luggage of his boss, a British *Bimbashi* (major) of the Sudan Defence Force, who was in a third following car, and that he had to hurry on to the railway station. The watchmen gave them permission to pass and Almasy took one of them on his running board to show the turn-off to the *Markaz*. He stopped, let the watchman off, and went on his way.

In the glow of the rising sun we drive through the most beautiful of all oases. On our right is the temple of Isis, then on the left the early Christian necropolis, the Roman citadel and the small watch towers and in between the most glorious spots of oasis with its bright green fields, the great shady *lebah* trees and the countless palms. The road is excellent.

Fifty kilometres on, at the crest of a steep Roman road in the Yabsa Pass, Almasy stopped to have his photograph taken, standing – bony and beaky-looking, his Afrika Korps shirt and shorts crumpled and desert-stained – beside a sign warning in English and Arabic, 'Dangerous descent – Drive in Bottom Gear'. Despite the warning he found the road was excellent, 'having enormously good effect on petrol consumption', and 'seems little frequented'.

At two that afternoon, driving with Pit, Pan and Munz while the other two remained behind in concealment to await his return, Almasy reached the edge of the Egyptian Plateau and within sight of Assiut.

Scarcely 4 km below us lies the huge green valley with the silver glittering river, the large white city, the countless *esbahs* [farms] and country houses. Not many words are said, a few handshakes, one last photograph, a short farewell and then I am driving back on our own tracks with Munz.

As Almasy drove off, Eppler and Sandstette trudged down the road towards the railway station on the edge of town, posing as travellers whose car had broken down. According to Eppler's later account they passed through a British military camp straddling the road to Assiut and were so convincing that they were invited into the officers' mess where they were given a shot of whisky and lunch before being sent on their way with good wishes.

Carrying two suitcases – one of them containing 'Sandy's' transceiver – they waited at Assiut railway station for the next up train to Cairo. It was 23 May and they had been trekking across the desert for eleven days. Operation Salam was accomplished; Operation Kondor was about to begin.

Chapter 18

Despite Jean Alington's self-imposed vigil at Bletchley Park and the best efforts of the 8th Army's Y (radio reconnaissance) Service in the field, a vital month was lost before the heads of cipher headquarters were able to read the Operation Salam intercepts and pass the information on to General Headquarters in Cairo.

As a consequence the British were not able, as she had hoped, to follow Almasy's course across the desert and alert the Long Range Desert Group to find him. This crucial information gap was partly due to the repeated failure of Almasy's own radio operator to get through to Schildkrote with messages in the Abwehr hand code which the British could intercept and decrypt; partly due to the sheer volume of Enigma traffic – much of it of far higher priority – that was passing through Bletchley Park daily; and, some suspected, partly due to the bureaucratic lassitude of the 'Long Range Shepheard's Group' in Cairo – the staff officers who seemed to spend much of their time lunching and drinking at the luxurious Shepheard's Hotel.*

Thus, it was not until 25 May that GHQ Cairo learned of Almasy's amended route via Kufra, the Gilf Kebir and

---

* Burned to the ground in the city-wide rioting that accompanied the 1952 revolution which overthrew King Farouk.

Kharga to Assiut, by which time he had dropped off Pit and Pan and was well on his way back to base. Even at that late date the LRDG at Kufra might have been able to intercept Almasy as he drove through Wadi el Aqaba on his way back to Jalo. But all Kufra's LRDG patrols were out searching for the wreckage of three South African Air Force Blenheim bombers that had gone missing while on a training flight in the vicinity three weeks before. It was not until 5 June, when the search had been called off, that a joint LRDG–SDF patrol led by Captain Ken Lazarus was sent to look for Almasy. They made straight for Wadi el Aqaba, but fresh vehicle tracks, west to east and east to west, made it clear to Lazarus that Almasy had already been and gone. Somewhat pointlessly, the patrol laid mines in the narrowest part of the wadi and set up an observation post to watch for the horse that had already bolted.

Not that Almasy's return trip had been without its moments of tension. Passing through Kharga again on 24 May he spotted one of the two watchmen he had en-countered on the way in. In his rear-view mirror he could see the *ghaffir* running after him. Questioned later, this man would tell the British about the strange vehicle that had passed through in both directions on successive days.

Despite this close call, Almasy felt confident enough to note in his diary that evening that 'it does not seem necessary to disappear too quickly into the desert. I can spare myself a good bit of miserable terrain if I just drive on along the Kharga–Dakhla road and turn off just before Dakhla to the south, to disappear into the great void.'

Almasy's immediate concern was to find the cache of

petrol he had left on the way out. Drifting sand had covered his tyre tracks and he lost sight of them several times. Eventually he recognized a familiar group of rocks and found the cleft where he had hidden the vital fuel. Amid the petrol cans was an unexpected intruder.

A large snake has found its way into a crack above the hiding place and looks at us with glowing emerald eyes. Munz wants to kill it, but I tell him that it is the *djinn* of our hiding place and hence of our return journey, too, which visibly impresses the men.

On 25 May, while approaching 'The Great Break', as he now termed the Wadi el Aqaba, Almasy's team saw the tracks of another snake, 'as thick as your arm'. Munz wanted to drive after it straight away to kill it, 'but I say that this time it is the *djinn* of the Gilf Kebir and that according to what the caravan leaders believe we have to meet yet a third in order to get home safely'.

Before camping for the night in the wadi, Almasy laid out an aircraft landing strip near its entrance 'to serve for an operation against the starting point of the enemy supply line'. The next morning he went to the spot where he had hidden the empty petrol drums taken from the parked British lorries he had found on the way in and painted in big letters on one of them: 'This is not el Aqaba. The pass lies 2.3 miles further east. Don't try! Most difficult to turn further up.'

'If another Tommy patrol should come looking for this pass,' he gloated in a diary note, 'the men will be grateful for this "accurate" information.' It was now the afternoon of 26 May and there were still ten days to go before the British mounted a full-scale search for him.

Later that day, en route to the Drei Burgen where he and his men had cached the 500 litres of petrol they had siphoned off from the British lorries' tanks, Almasy spotted in the plain below three enemy motorized columns a few kilometres apart from each other and totalling more than seventy vehicles. They were supply columns, not combat patrols, but nevertheless presented a serious danger.

One column had stopped right in front of the entrance to the Bab el Misr, his 'Gateway to Egypt'. The other two columns were heading in the same direction. 'We have to get out of the mountains via the *Bab el Misr* pass before these columns,' said Almasy, and he moved off 'in a state of alert with MG [machine-gun] ready to open up'. In concealment from above he could see the first vehicles of the second column appearing on the skyline, barely four kilometres behind the leading column.

Meanwhile, twenty-eight vehicles of the first column were deployed opposite the entrance to the pass, effectively blocking Almasy's way in: 'We are cut off . . . What shall I do now? On the narrow mountain track between here and *Bab el Misr* there is no chance of evasion.'

Almasy decided that only the boldest bluff could save them from capture. Leading his three vehicles down into the plain, he ordered his men to 'close all windows and follow quite quickly and just behind me. No shooting; at most salute.' Then he handed his Leica camera to Woehrmann, saying: 'Take a photo in passing. I'll lean back so that you can make the exposure past me.'

I drove so as to leave [the enemy] on my right; the sun was deep down on the left so they could hardly recognize the markings on our vehicles. I saluted with the hand raised and the Sudanese rose to return the salute . . . We had to proceed quite slowly on account of the stony ground and Woehrmann took 6 exposures . . . This quaint meeting was over in a few seconds . . .

They passed through the Bab el Misr without incident until, exactly 7 miles (12 km.) on, Almasy's left back tyre was punctured: 'Good job that it did not happen near the enemy column!' Once the tyre was fixed, the safe return of the Almasy Commando seemed assured, even though the men 'were gradually showing signs of exhaustion', there was much hard driving ahead and they narrowly missed bumping into a three-car enemy patrol near Bir Abu Zereigh at the northern edge of the Kufra Oasis.

Exactly at noon on 29 May they reached the southern edge of the Jalo airfield, fired three white flares to warn of their arrival, hoisted the Italian tricolour on their aerial mast and drove in – a triumph for Almasy and a telling, if unique, rebuff to the LRDG in their own back yard.

Bill Kennedy Shaw for one was forced to concede subsequently that Operation Salam had been 'a good effort . . . worthy of Almasy's desert craft'. And when, a few days later, Almasy met Rommel in the field to report success, the *Panzerarmee* commander promoted him on the spot to major and awarded him an Iron Cross, First Class, to add to the Second Class cross he had already won.

But Rommel, though brilliant and dashing, was not really interested in unconventional warfare along the lines suggested by Almasy's successful operation and conducted by the British 'mosquito army'. He was entirely focused on smashing through the British defences with his armour and occupying the Nile Valley, Alexandria and Cairo. Against this grand strategic aim, Almasy's hopes of creating an LRDG of his own were irrelevant and never to be fulfilled. Within a few weeks, he would be on his way home to Hungary, bemedalled and promoted but ill and disappointed.

If Operation Salam was a brilliant success, Operation Kondor which followed was a dismal failure. Eppler and Sandstette made their way to Cairo easily enough and before long had set themselves up in a luxurious houseboat on the Nile at Zamalek, tended by a couple of Nubian servants. They had an alluring neighbour, a celebrated bellydancer named Hekmat Fahmy, who had been one of Eppler's many lady friends during his pre-war existence as Hussein Ghaffar, Cairene man-about-town.

Among Hekmat's current bedmates were a number of British staff officers and, according to Eppler's post-war memoirs, she and others of the belly-dancing sorority were only too willing to pass on, for appropriate payment, any interesting fragments of pillow talk they might pick up.

For his part, Eppler began to dispense the forged £5 notes provided by the Abwehr* in the clubs and bars where he hoped to overhear interesting loose talk. By hanging

---

* This was a serious mistake by the Abwehr: they should have known that British currency was not commonly in use in Egypt.

discreetly around 8th Army depots he was also able to see hundreds of new American Sherman tanks arriving daily for deployment to the front line, which by this time had moved to El Alamein, a mere 60 miles (100 km.) from Alexandria.

But none of the snippets of information that Eppler was able to glean were getting through to Rommel's head-quarters: Sandstette was again unable to make radio contact with Schildkrote or either of the two alternative stations the Abwehr had set up. Thinking the problem might lie in his equipment he called in help from the Egyptian Army, whose younger officers were hoping that an Axis victory would bring them freedom from the British. A twenty-two-year-old signals lieutenant named Anwar Sadat came to check out the spies' transceiver but found nothing wrong with it.

He did, however, find much to deplore in Pit and Pan's lifestyle. Their houseboat was 'a place straight out of the *Thousand and One Nights*', the future president of Egypt would recall, 'where everything invited indolence, vol-uptuousness and pleasure of the senses'. On a later visit to the houseboat he was even more shocked to find the two spies 'dead drunk in the company of two Jewish women'.*

Meanwhile, British security were on the spies' trail. They

---

* In later years, when he was President of Egypt, Sadat was markedly less puritanical, taking undisguised pleasure in his hand-rolled cigars, single-malt Scotch whiskies and Savile Row suits. He also, of course, went to Jerusalem, publicly embraced Israeli Prime Minister Mena-chem Begin and his predecessor Golda Meier, and in due course signed the Camp David peace accords, ending Egypt's state of war with Israel.

had already been warned by Bletchley Park that there were a couple of German agents in the city and a raid by an Australian unit on a German radio interception station near El Alamein on 7 July had closed down Schildkrote and produced an unexpected and initially puzzling bonus: two copies in English of Daphne du Maurier's best-selling novel, *Rebecca*. On investigation this book turned out to be the intended key to the decrypting of Pit and Pan's transmissions.

The net was closing. In the small hours of 25 July a team from British Field Security surrounded the spies' houseboat and seized them before they could scuttle the vessel. Under interrogation Pit and Pan told all, including the help they had received from Lieutenant Sadat, a disclosure that led to his immediate arrest and probably saved their lives.

Although it was routine practice on all sides to execute captured enemy agents, the British realized it might be politically counter-productive to hang Sadat together with Eppler and Sandstette. At this crucial point, with Rommel almost literally hammering at the gates, to execute an Egyptian officer might well have caused great unrest or even a general uprising. Thus all three lived to tell the tale, Eppler and Sadat in best-selling if self-serving post-war memoirs.*

Summing up the affair of the 'Houseboat Spies', as they were to be called by the British media, a report to the War Office by military intelligence seemed only to confirm Almasy's impression of Eppler and Sandstette as something

---

*Sadat, *Revolt on the Nile*; Eppler, *Operation Condor: Rommel's Spy*. See Bibliography.

of a comedy duo: They had 'spent most of their time and money in riotous living', said the report, and it was 'partly through their own carelessness . . . that they were arrested'.

Chapter 19

In mid August of 1942, as the British 8th Army manned the defences at El Alamein and the pro-German majority in Alexandria and Cairo prepared to greet a conquering Rommel with cheers and embraces, Almasy left North Africa for medical treatment in Nazi-occupied Athens. He was suffering from an acute form of amoebic dysentery, picked up during his epic 2,600-mile trek across the desert to Assiut and back.

Rommel's personal congratulations on the success of Operation Salam, the two Iron Crosses on his chest and the major's insignia on the shoulders of his Luftwaffe uniform were all very well, but the ludicrous failure of Operation Kondor must have rankled, as had the knowledge that he was no longer needed in the desert.

Rommel had made it clear that he had no interest in sponsoring a rival LRDG and Almasy's value to the Abwehr might well expire on his release from hospital. To add to his despondency was the parting from Hans Entholt. Fully recovered from his own illness, and now no longer an officer candidate but a sub-lieutenant, Entholt had returned to North Africa in July to a junior post on Rommel's staff.

As they exchanged farewells, Almasy could console himself with the thought that at least Entholt had been

193

spared the greater dangers of the Eastern Front and the hope
that before long they might be together again.

On his discharge from hospital in Athens, Almasy opted
to return to Hungary via Italy. He had decided to renew
his acquaintanceship with Pat Clayton – and traced him to
a prisoner-of-war camp near Sulmona in the Abruzzi region
of Italy – to talk over old times and perhaps to boast a little
about how he had beaten the LRDG at their own game
and on their own turf. The camp commandant allowed him
to take Clayton to a local *trattoria* for a drink, either on his
own recognizance or on Clayton's parole.

One post-war German account describes Almasy as
'gloating' as he told 'his old buddy' about the success of
Operation Salam, adding that Clayton 'gritted his teeth' at
the news. Clayton himself had a rather different interpretation of his reaction, as Peter Clayton would write in a
memoir of his father.

The remarks about Pat gritting his teeth were more likely to
have been due to Almasy's remembered habit, Pat said later, of
leaving someone else (him on this occasion!) to pay the bill for
the refreshments ordered. Almasy was nevertheless able to block
Pat's transfer to the notorious Campo Cinque, the Italian high
security POW camp equivalent of Colditz,* and arrange instead
for him to go to Campo 29 Veano in Northern Italy . . . This
was appreciated and very much worth the price of a couple of
drinks!

* Another example of the influence Almasy appeared to wield in senior
Axis circles. Colditz Castle was the grim camp where the Germans
kept incorrigible escapers.

18. Almasy's vehicle on a hard surface at Ain Doua. The spring emerges in the rocks behind the car

19. Almasy dwarfed by the entrance to the Cave of the Swimmers. Inside he found prehistoric paintings of swimming men

20, 21. Watercolours from Almasy's sketchbook of the cave paintings at Wadi Soura. *Left*, the swimmers and a prehistoric handprint; *below*, archers doing battle

22, 23. In 1935 a fellow desert pioneer, Bill Kennedy Shaw, photographed these cave paintings of domesticated cattle

24. The Italian military headquarters at Kufra as photographed by Almas in 1932

25. The massive Gilf Kebir escarpment overshadows Almasy and his Ford Model A

26. Ralph Bagnold's men meet a motorized Italian patrol on reconnaissance at Ain Doua

27, 28. Almasy photographed during Operation Salam. *Right*, he stands by a British military warning sign on the approach to Assiut; *below*, with the two German spies 'Pit and Pan' and two members of the Brandenburg Regiment in front of the Cave of the Swimmers

29. Home of the Almasy family. Burg Bernstein seen from the air

30. Almasy's older brother Janos seated left with Unity Mitford, his wife Princess Maria Rosa in her wheelchair and a friend on the lawn at Burg Bernstein, *c.* 1936

31. Almasy in his uniform as a captain of the Hungarian Air Force Reserve, 1939

32. The People's Court document acquitting Almasy of charges of war crimes, 23 November 1946

While they had a convivial drink Almasy may have said more than he should, for soon after his visit Clayton wrote home using a code prearranged by British intelligence for use by selected officer POWs. The letter contained 'many strange references' which baffled Clayton's wife, Ellie, but she dutifully passed it on to MI9 at the War Office. This and other of Clayton's otherwise mundane letters (*'I received your parcel today . . . A few bad days' weather but now it has cleared up'*) contained a mysterious reference to 'Peter's little sister Dora'. This must have been a hidden message, since Peter had no sister and there was later discovered to be an Abwehr operation code-named Dora, aimed at disrupting the Allies' aerial supply line from the Gulf of Guinea, across equatorial Africa to Port Sudan. Almasy would presumably have known about this plan and one must speculate whether, inadvertently or otherwise, he had let something slip about it to Clayton.

Operation Dora, involving a force of one hundred Brandenburgers and commanded by a Lieutenant von Leipzig, was launched from Tripoli in July 1942. They travelled south through the western Sahara in twenty-four heavily armed captured British vehicles. All the men of this special force unit were fluent in either English or French and three were Arabic-speakers. Their chosen sphere of operations was around Lake Chad and, according to post-war accounts, they soon came to believe that the Arabs of the region hated the French and were sympathetic to the Axis. Had Almasy rather than Leipzig been in command he might have warned his men of the desert Arab's tendency to tell strangers what they imagined they would like to hear.

However that might be, the three patrols into which Leipzig divided his force soon ran into unexpectedly heavy resistance from the Free French garrison. And as Almasy had found during Operation Salam, the Brandenburgers were not always quite what they were cracked up to be. Before long they were limping back to Tripoli with their wounded, mission unaccomplished.

After the war – and following his father's death in 1962 – Peter Clayton remained unable to decipher this correspondence, even using published details of the POW code.

From his meeting with Clayton in the Abruzzi, Almasy went on to Germany, where he reported to Major Seubert, his Abwehr superior, and requested to be put on the reserve list, citing ill health and advancing years. He was about to turn forty-seven.

Back in Budapest, hard up as usual in his well-off, patrician way, Almasy began writing a brief memoir of the North African campaign, *With Rommel's Army in Libya*. It was published in Budapest the following January, bringing him in a little much-needed income – and also a good deal of unanticipated trouble for the future.

The manuscript was, of course, vetted by the Abwehr, and censored before publication, by the Nazi Propaganda Ministry. As published it contained no mention of the name of Major Ritter, nor any of Almasy's comrades, nor of the Almasy Commando, nor of Operation Salam. Those deletions were obviously for security reasons. For propaganda reasons, the book was sprinkled with phrases like 'brave German lads' and 'blond German boys' – and in one place Almasy finds it 'touching to see how [in contrast to the vandalizing enemy] the German troops tried to leave the settler houses in good condition'. This tendentious stuff sounds less like Almasy than Dr Goebbels' zealots enhancing the original.

This is undoubtedly the case when they have Almasy gushing about 'these blue-eyed blond German boys who have only been in Africa a few months, yet they act as though the only life they've ever known is that of a long range desert scout'. How different from the opinion of his 20 May 1942 entry in the Operation Salam diary: 'All in all, with the exception of Munz, these men have no talent for driving . . . What a difference compared to my Sudanese!'

Under the deliberately non-specific chapter heading 'Desert Patrol' and the dateline May 1942, the published memoir describes some episodes of Operation Salam without naming it or giving any hint as to what it was all about. This chapter does, however, provide some insights into Almasy's hard-won desert craft.

Our three vehicles are parked in staggered fashion, facing north into the wind. There is a reason for this. Fire is the greatest hazard . . . Every vehicle carries enough fuel for several thousand kilometres, we cook on Primus stoves and in addition some of us smoke. We need to make sure that in case of fire the flames don't leap from car to car. Since the desert air is so dry a cigarette spark can ignite a seat cushion or a piece of clothing. One must be extremely cautious around the petrol cans, which are always condensing. If we spend more than one night at the same spot we unload the cans and place them beyond the reach of any windswept sparks.

Beyond such practical considerations, Almasy finds poetry in the banal routines of camp, instancing 'the rhythmic knock of the Primus pump and soon afterwards the angry hiss of the flame'.

Over many years, through countless nights, this has become such a familiar sound. It's as much part of camp life, the desert, Africa, as the star-filled firmament, the sigh of the wind, the creaking of the sand under our footsteps. It's strange, this monotone hissing, suggestive of stifled strength, energy, life . . .

On Easter Sunday 1942, when Almasy is visiting the Italian garrison at Jalo, he is invited to attend a special mass. The troops faced the altar in an open rectangle and 'listened to the holy mass with the same reverence one finds in our old village churches back home'.

The words of the gospel sound so different in these surroundings, as though the mystery of Easter has penetrated more deeply into our souls. It occurs to me that the words of the Resurrection are being heard for the first time on this spot. The war brought them to us in this hidden oasis where our presence has disturbed a thousand years of peace.

While at Jalo, Almasy sent a message to Haj Mohammed Taher, a leading member of the local Zuwaiya Senussi, mentioning a mutual friend of pre-war days, the Oxford-educated Egyptian court official Hassanein Bey. Taher replied with an invitation to his home. Almasy put on his cleanest uniform and conscientiously left behind his cigarettes and lighter. 'It would have been discourteous to violate the Senussi prohibition against smoking in the home of a holy man.'

Haj Taher's house may have been larger and more spacious than the average one in the village, but its interior arrangement was similar. A large reception area with a columned porch opened onto a third courtyard. The beaten clay floor was covered with colourful rugs, most of them woven on Bedouin looms by women in the Misratah region. There were also some genuine Turkish and Persian rugs. Along the full length of the windowless wall facing the entrance there was a low adobe bench covered with soft pillows and fine carpets. My host took his centre place and seated me to his right. Only then did he introduce his grown grandsons.

After an exchange of the customary Arabic courtesies, quietly murmured, hand to breast, they talk of this and that and of their mutual friend Hassanein, now elevated from bey to pasha.* They drink several cups of strong, bitter tea brewed at the table by Almasy's host with water from a distant well renowned for its quality. Then Taher asks a question 'which causes my heart to skip a beat'.

In Egypt did I meet a man who travelled a lot in the desert and was called *Abu Ramleh*, the 'father of the sands'? On the one hand I'm flattered that word of me has spread even to this desolate

---

* Roughly analogous to promotion from lord to prince.

oasis, since I was honoured with this name many years ago, but I can't reveal to my host that *Abu Ramleh* is his guest. The intelligence service of the oases is secretive and inscrutable and it would not be advisable for the local population to know my true identity.

Almasy's description of his first encounter with Rommel, the German commander he had been instructed to work *with*, but not *for*, reflects something of the respect, verging on hero worship, the man so widely inspired, not just among his own troops but the enemy, too.

Rommel is a muscular, straight-backed man of medium height, with a gaze that is always serious, almost stern. Though 50 years old, his appearance is youthful, his movements determined, and his voice firm. His bearing does not betray the strain of the almost superhuman challenges he faces and the weight of the huge responsibilities he shoulders. He speaks calmly and unemotionally, but rarely smiles. He sometimes jokes with the soldiers but is always serious with the officers.★

Even in a text passed and approved by Nazi censors, Almasy is allowed to question the morality of war in the desert. 'I can somehow comprehend combat on the dreary Russian steppe, but here under the African sky, in the world of the oases – the genuine symbols of peace and mystery – how can men murder one another?'

Not long after publication, Almasy received news that

★ Following the July 1944 plot to assassinate Hitler, Rommel was forced to swallow a lethal cyanide pill to protect his family and preserve his heroic reputation.

cast him into deep despair: Entholt had been killed in a land-mine explosion as Rommel's army withdrew across North Africa following the crucial British victory at El Alamein. Almasy was devastated. In a diary note that seems to embody all the 'loving and longing' Entholt had spoken of in an earlier letter, and all the insecurities that lurked behind the assured façade of the seasoned desert adventurer, Almasy wrote:

Seven years of the most exquisite closeness have I poisoned with my doubts, my fears of being a burden, my material dependency! Then this terrible thing hit me as cruelly as any man can be hit. Since then everything has seemed banal, empty and sad.★

The Abwehr had not entirely finished with Almasy. In November 1943, according to which account one believes, they sent him either to the Crimea on unspecified duties or to neutral Turkey to liaise with his prominent pro-German Egyptian friends of pre-war days. Another unverifiable (but by no means unbelievable) account of his activities during this period suggests that while in Turkey, or subsequently, he was 'turned' by British intelligence and became a double agent. If so, his case was not unique: it is a matter of record that during the winter of 1943–4 three other Abwehr agents in Istanbul *did* defect to the Allies.

Entholt's death may have been sufficient to convince Almasy of the futility of Hitler's war while later events do, indeed, suggest that at some point Almasy might have felt an even better reason to change sides.

★ For attribution, see footnote, page 132, Chapter 12.

From late 1943 to March 1944, his trail goes cold, for lack of credible documentary or even attributable anecdotal evidence as to his precise whereabouts and activities. The British historian Saul Kelly,★ an indefatigable researcher, has unearthed German documents which link a character, referred to only as 'Teddy', to a complicated scheme to infiltrate German agents by air into North Africa after the mass surrender of Axis forces at Tunis in the spring of 1943. Could 'Teddy' have been Almasy? Possibly, but the link seems inconclusive and in detail the scheme itself seems more than a little hare-brained.

However that may be, Almasy's connections with the Abwehr must have been shaken if not entirely disrupted in March 1944, when the Germans turned on their ally, Hungary, and sent an occupation force across the frontier from Austria to keep it in line. The Third Reich had learned that Horthy, at best an equivocal friend, had 'betrayed' them by sending out secret feelers for a separate peace with the advancing Russians – an offence he would later compound by insisting that the Germans stop deporting 'his' Jews to the extermination camps of occupied Poland.

Like most of the Magyar ruling elite, Horthy had arm's length contacts with but was no great lover of Hungary's thriving, comparatively well-integrated and partially assimilated Jewish minority. They had played a disproportionately large role in Hungary's business, professional, scientific and cultural life, some achieving high social status, but

★ In his *The Search for Zerzura*. See Bibliography.

Magyar gentlemen of pure blood on the whole disdained commerce, the arts and the professions in favour of more 'manly' pursuits. Nevertheless, Horthy was no fanatic on the 'Jewish Question' and for all his fascistic, man-on-a-white-horse posturing he drew the line well short of mass murder.

Before the Germans lost patience with him and sent their troops into Hungary, there had been three-quarters of a million Jews in the country, many of them refugees from Poland, to whom Hungary seemed a relatively safe haven in a murderously hostile continent. But with the field-grey invaders who crossed the frontier from Austria came the black-clad *Sondereinsatzkommando* (special action group) of SS Colonel Adolf Eichmann, the managing director, so to speak, of Hitler's genocidal 'travel bureau'. They set to work with the zeal that many years later was to send Eichmann to the gallows in Israel. Four months after their arrival only the Jews of the capital remained, waiting in hiding or in improvised detention camps to be deported to the Nazi death factories.

At about this time two things happened: Horthy insisted that the fate of Hungary's Jews was a matter for *his* government, and a young Swede named Raoul Wallenberg arrived in Budapest by train, armed only with diplomatic credentials and a puny handgun to defend himself. Wallenberg's American-sponsored mission, fully backed by the neutral Swedish government, was to thwart Eichmann's genocidal plans by any means available. It must have seemed a hopeless task.

Horthy, still Hungary's nominal head of state, had been

bombarded with pleas and warnings from, among others, US President Franklin Roosevelt, Pope Pius XII and International Red Cross President Karl Burckhardt. They unanimously appealed to his sense of honour and Christian decency to protect Hungary's remaining Jews, Roosevelt adding the threat of retribution – immediate or post-war – if he failed to do so.

To give teeth to his policy of trying to save the remnants of Europe's Jews, Roosevelt had established the War Refugee Board, whose representative in Stockholm had chosen Wallenberg, descendant of a distinguished Swedish diplomatic, banking and naval family, with a free hand to direct the board's operations in Hungary.

By the time Wallenberg arrived, Horthy had plucked up the courage to tell his German 'guests' that he could no longer allow the deportations: 440,000 Jews had already been sent to Auschwitz by cattle truck from the Hungarian provinces, some three hundred thousand remained trapped in Budapest and Horthy, acutely conscious that the Allies were advancing towards the German heartland from both east and west, had decided it was time to start mending fences.

He sent back to the provinces the sixty thousand Hungarian gendarmes who had been deployed in the capital as manpower for Eichmann. Enraged by this 'treachery', but having far too few SS men on hand to round up and deport so many Jews unaided, Eichmann had to accept the situation. For the time being.

Taking advantage of the lull in deportations, Wallenberg, under his cover as First Secretary of the Swedish Legation, began to prepare frantically and innovatively for the next wave of deportations, which he guessed was bound to come. Knowing how anxious Horthy's beleaguered government was to gain 'respectability' and international recognition, he reminded all concerned that Sweden represented Hungarian interests in a number of capitals at a time when the tide of war was turning decisively against the Axis.

He was well aware that individual Hungarians in high places were increasingly susceptible to threats of post-war retribution and promises of Swedish good offices, according to how they behaved now. Wallenberg was quite prepared to descend to bribery and blackmail, if necessary, to achieve his ends and had ample funds at his disposal for the greasing of palms.

His first move was to design, print and issue thousands of impressive looking, multicoloured *Schutzpassen* – fake passports ostensibly giving the holder the protection of the Swedish crown. Surprisingly often, they worked.* Emboldened by Wallenberg's example, other neutral legations began to follow suit. The Swiss apparently issued even more passes than the Swedes. Next, Wallenberg leased a number of substantial buildings around the city, flew the Swedish flag prominently over them, and housed his passport-holders inside. He also set up clinics, nurseries and soup kitchens and before long had a staff of four hundred, mostly Jews, working for his department at the Swedish Legation.

* A Hungarian Holocaust survivor in Stockholm once told the author: 'We'd see an Orthodox Jew in the street – black hat, beard, side-locks and all – and we'd say "Look, there goes another Swede."'

Ultimately, he relied on bravado and sheer nerve to cajole and bully the lower and middle ranks of the enemy. These tactics did not work with Eichmann himself who, watching and waiting for his chance, even tried to have Wallenberg assassinated by ramming his car with a heavy German army truck.

It was against this background that a period of uneasy calm began while deportations were suspended. Then Hitler's patience snapped and the Nazis lunged again. To ensure Horthy's future compliance with his plans for genocide, and his loyalty in the war against the Soviets, Hitler had the Regent's son kidnapped by a Waffen SS unit under the notorious Colonel Otto Skorzeny. The younger Horthy was drugged, rolled up in an antique carpet in the forecourt of Buda Castle, bundled into a van and spirited away to Germany.

The senior Horthy caved in and was himself taken to Germany as a virtual prisoner. Then the Germans installed a Hungarian government more to their liking – that of the home-grown Nazi Party, the Arrow Cross, who if anything were even more enthusiastically anti-semitic than their German role models.

The stage was now set for Almasy to emerge in a role that casts him in a rather better light than his detractors might allow. As a Hungarian patriot of the old school, he was undoubtedly shocked by the brutal and peremptory German take-over of his country and although the option to take up arms against the invader did not exist, it may well be that this was the point at which he decided to make his individual peace with the Allies and become a double agent.

Additionally, there was one small but morally significant way in which – if he should choose – he could salve his conscience and hinder the plans of the invader.

Chapter 20

Budapest in the closing months of 1944 was a nightmarish city. The US Air Force bombed it by day, the Royal Air Force bombed it by night, and from the east the rolling thunder of Soviet artillery heralded the steady advance of the Red Army, lighting up the horizon at night with the flashes of their heavy guns.

The population were starving. Household pets had become commodities for the pot and hungry citizens fell upon and butchered the corpses of horses, killed in the streets by artillery and bomb bursts.

With the resumption of the Jewish deportations, the morale of the Eichmann Commando was high. Undeterred by a critical shortage of railway cattle cars to carry thousands of Jews to the gas chambers of Auschwitz, Eichmann ruled that if they could not ride they must walk. So began a series of notorious death marches from Budapest to the Austrian border at Hegyeshalom, 120 miles away, in which hundreds of men, women and children perished in the ice and snow of a particularly harsh winter.

When, a couple of days before Christmas 1944, Eichmann and his men bolted for home at the approach of the Red Army, the Arrow Cross 'death brigades' enthusiastically took over sole administration of Hungary's Final Solution, replacing the cold process of transportation to distant death camps with an unrestrained orgy of on-the-spot rape, torture and murder. One night they even invaded a Jewish orphanage, slaughtering every child within while a Roman Catholic chaplain, wearing a death's-head armband, pronounced a benediction on their efforts.

And the Arrow Cross Interior Minister, Gabor Vajna, warned in a radio broadcast that 'this solution [of the 'Jewish Problem'], even if it shall be ruthless, shall be such as the Jews deserve by their present and previous conduct'.

I recognize no Jews belonging to the Roman Catholic or Lutheran churches. I recognize no letter of safe conduct of any kind or foreign passport which a Jew of Hungarian nationality may have received from whatever source or person . . . Let not a single person of Jewish race believe then that with the help of aliens he can circumvent the lawful measures of the Hungarian State.

A favoured Arrow Cross method of disposing of the Jews of Budapest was to round up groups of them and, after some 'sport' in their district torture rooms, march them down shackled together in threes to the Danube. From his ground-floor flat in the four-storey Almasy mansion on fashionable Miklos Horthy Avenue, Almasy had a grandstand view of this daily Via Dolorosa as the victims were driven at gunpoint past the smart shops and the grand family mansions to their captors' execution spot of choice – the embankment opposite the *grand luxe* Gellert Hotel, a couple of hundred yards from Almasy's flat.

There the Arrow Cross men would force their victims down the stone steps, line them up on the river bank and shoot one of each three, who would fall into the river and drag the others in after him. For this no benediction was necessary; the fast-flowing Danube washed away the sin and, anyway, it would not do to pollute the air of Budapest's most fashionable quarter with the stench of rotting corpses.

During the horrific autumn/winter of 1944 we know of two cases in which, at some risk to himself, Almasy intervened to save the lives of individual Jews. The authenticity of these two cases is supported by solid documentary evidence. There is also a third case which is supported only by anec- dotal evidence, and that from a person who may have had a familial axe to grind. This case concerns a Polish-Jewish boy, aged eight or nine, named Rubinstein, reputedly the nephew of the celebrated concert pianist, Artur Rubinstein.

As Almasy's niece Zita Gyomyorey, daughter of his sister Gyorgina, related some years after the event, the Rubinstein child's parents were seized during a round-up of Jews in the late autumn of 1944. Somehow the little boy evaded capture and found a hiding place in the Danube resort town of Leanyfalu, north of Budapest. Learning of his presence there, alone and in great peril, Zita alerted her uncle.

Wearing his Luftwaffe uniform and medals, Zita claimed, Almasy drove her to the scene in his pre-war grey Lincoln saloon, blustering his way through an Arrow Cross road- block en route. As Zita told it, the big American car, the aristocratic mien of its owner and his German uniform were quite enough to intimidate the militiamen at the checkpoint.

At Leanyfalu, Almasy and his niece extricated the terrified boy from his hiding place, put him on the back seat of the

Lincoln and covered him with a blanket before passing through the same roadblock and driving on to Budapest. There, according to his niece, Almasy hid the boy in his flat while he acquired false identity papers for him under the impeccably Aryan name of Arkos Antal.

Although the Hungarian gendarmerie and Arrow Cross police were breaking into houses and apartments everywhere, looking for hidden Jews, Almasy calculated that they would be unlikely to invade the privacy of a man known to have fought for the Germans and to have won the Iron Cross. After a few days, according to Zita, she and her uncle took the boy to Budapest West railway station and handed him over to an unnamed friend, wearing Hungarian Army officer's uniform.

This man in turn took the boy on to Vac, a nearby town, where he was given refuge in the Don Bosco Roman Catholic school or orphanage. There, in the care of the Salesian Brothers, young Rubinstein survived the war and was eventually reunited with relatives in the United States. From his new home he reputedly kept in touch with his benefactors by mail for some years.

There are two things wrong with this account, which was given by Zita Gyomyorey to the geographer and Almasy biographer, Janos Kubassek: Artur Rubinstein never had a nephew remotely answering to the description of 'Arkos Antal' and it seems that there never was a Don Bosco school, orphanage or refuge of any kind at Vac.

The maestro's two children – John Rubinstein in Los Angeles and Eva Rubinstein in New York – both assured the author that, although many of their relatives had been caught up in the Holocaust, no such cousin had gone from Poland to Hungary or had later come to America. Neither did the maestro himself, in his two volumes of autobiography published in the 1970s, make any reference to any such relative or incident. His only known nephew had been born in France, some years before the rise of Hitler.

That discrepancy alone may not necessarily give the lie to Zita Gyomyorey's account: Rubinstein is a common enough Jewish family name and she might honestly have believed, or convinced herself, that the boy was related to the great pianist. But detailed searches in Hungarian Episcopal and state archives have turned up no trace of a Don Bosco establishment of any kind in Vac either before, during or after the war. Thus, the authenticity of the Rubinstein 'rescue' must, at the least, remain doubtful.

Not so, however, another case which concerns Almasy and a Jew named Jeno Fuchs, in his day Hungary's most outstanding if controversial international sporting figure. It is not clear whether or not Almasy had met Fuchs before he saved him and his family from deportation, but like every Hungarian of his generation he must have known of him, for in his youth Fuchs had brought home no fewer than four Olympic gold medals.

As pieced together from official Olympic Committee publications, entries in biographical reference books, oral recollections gathered by Dr Kubassek and – seeming conclusively to confirm Almasy's part in it – the official record of certain post-war court proceedings in Budapest, this is the remarkable story of Jeno Fuchs.

As a university student in Budapest around the end of
the nineteenth century, he set himself a hitherto unusual
goal for one of Jewish birth – to beat his loftily anti-semitic
fellow students at their own game, the sabre. Defying the
notion that fencing was a pastime reserved exclusively for
Magyar gentlemen,★ a ruling that only members of author-
ized, Jew-excluding fencing clubs could take part in national
competitions, and a widespread perception that Jews were
anyway fit for nothing more strenuous than commerce, the
professions and the arts, he set out to prove them wrong
on all three counts. Other Jewish students followed his
example and fencing became something of a popular passion
among them. When challenged to a duel their anti-semitic
tormentors were honour-bound to respond.

Fuchs certainly did not look the part of a champion
swordsman. He was 'physically unimposing – short, balding
and wore glasses', according to an officially sponsored
Olympic Committee report. But he was driven. Practising
privately and training relentlessly, he made such outstanding
progress that in pre-Olympic trials he gave the Hungarian
Olympic Committee, deeply divided but hungry for gold,
little option but to send him to the 1908 Games in London,
not only as an individual competitor but as captain of the
national sabre team.

★ 'This martial upper-class sport seemed inappropriate for Jews, who
had been barred from bearing arms in the nineteenth century.' According to *Olympika: The International Journal of Olympic Studies* (vol. V,
1996, pp. 151–8), 'Jewish interest in the sport began among university
students who learned to fence so they could challenge anti-semitic
classmates to duels.'

There he won every contest he undertook, winning an individual gold medal and a team gold as skipper of the Hungarian sabre squad. Four years later, at the Stockholm Olympics, he repeated the process, finishing his international career at the age of thirty with four gold medals to his name. He had put Hungary on the sporting map as a major force in fencing and the official *Swedish Olympic Report* wrote:

The Hungarians . . . brilliantly maintained their reputation as perhaps the greatest masters of the sabre in Europe and their leading representative Dr Fuchs awakened general admiration by the skill and strength he displayed during the course of the competition. Although of slight build and rather low stature he succeeded by means of well-calculated sabre play in repelling the attacks of and defeating the most powerfully built and vigorous opponents.

Alas, the 'general admiration' did not extend to all of Fuchs's fellow citizens. Many among the Hungarian ruling elite (and a good many of less elevated social status) felt aggrieved that a mere Jew should excel at a sport they considered their own.*

---

* Fuchs was no flash in the pan. A fellow Hungarian Jew, Janos Garay, won an individual gold medal for the sabre in the 1928 Amsterdam Olympics, having already won a team bronze and an individual silver in 1924. He was also European sabre champion in 1925 and 1930. Garay died in 1945 in the Nazis' Mauthausen death camp. A third Hungarian Jewish sabre star, Dezso Foldes, was a member of Fuchs's winning teams in 1908 and 1912, after which he had the foresight to emigrate to the United States.

In a small office he rented in Zsibarus Street, on the Pest side of the Danube, the returning hero hung his Olympic citation on the wall alongside his law degree and, according to a 1993 *in memoriam* article by the leading Budapest sports journalist Gyorgy Szilagyi in the *Hungarian Olympic Bulletin*, 'waited for clients who didn't come'. Unmarried at the time, he lived in his parents' modest flat.

Despite his Olympic golds and his accolades abroad, Fuchs could never compete in Hungarian national events: to do so, he would have to belong to a registered fencing club and these – with one exception – did not admit Jews. The exception was a Jews-only sports club founded in 1908. But this club had a strong Zionist political connection and Fuchs, like many of his fellows at the time, was not a Zionist. He considered himself to be a Jewish Hungarian – as one might be a Catholic Hungarian or a Protestant Hungarian – rather than a Hungarian Jew. And in affirmation of his patriotism he rushed to the colours when, two years after his triumph at Stockholm, Austria–Hungary went to war.

The defeat of 1918 bringing the dismemberment of Austria–Hungary, followed by the Red Terror of Bela Kun's communists and the White Terror of Horthy's counter-revolutionaries, did nothing to enhance intercommunal relations. During the 1920s and 1930s anti-Jewish discrimination became institutionalized but Fuchs – by now married with a young son and working in the legal department of the Budapest Stock Exchange – remained a Hungarian first. He still considered himself a Hungarian patriot when, thirty years after his last Olympic triumph, his country joined Hitler's war against Russia.

Although he was now pushing sixty and past the age of
conscription into the all-Jewish forced labour battalions
Horthy was sending to the Eastern Front, Fuchs volunteered
to go. The labour battalions were not allowed to wear
uniform or carry arms. Their job was to dig trenches and
latrines and perform other menial tasks – generally under
appalling conditions – for the fighting troops. But Fuchs
took on an even more demanding and dangerous task as
section commander of a mine-laying and mine-sweeping
unit of the 3rd Hungarian Army Corps operating alongside
German forces in the vicinity of Stalingrad.

According to Szilagyi's impressively detailed account,
in an adjoining sector on the Don river front the Wehrmacht's 323rd Infantry Regiment was deployed under
the command of one Colonel Friedrich Trompeter,*
himself a fencer and pentathlon athlete of world class.
Fuchs's unit had been attached to this regiment, unarmed
and under the watchful eye of four German infantrymen in
case they should try to desert to the Russians. Although
Trompeter and Fuchs were unaware of each other's proximity they were old acquaintances. Trompeter had even
invited Fuchs as his personal guest to visit the 1936 Berlin
Olympics.

One day at his field headquarters in the late autumn of
1942 the colonel was astonished to read a report from one
of his best company commanders, a Captain Hoffmann: a

* Trompeter survived the Battle of Stalingrad and, according to the
records of the Wehrmacht's 305th Infantry Division, was awarded the
Knight's Cross, Germany's highest award for gallantry, in northern
Italy in January 1945.

Russian unit had attacked Fuchs's detachment, killing all four of its German minders, but, far from taking the opportunity to defect, Fuchs had ordered his men to seize the fallen Germans' weapons and repel the attack. They did so, Captain Hoffmann reported, and succeeded in driving the Russians off, saving a considerable amount of valuable mine-clearing equipment in the process.

Hoffmann recommenced that Fuchs should receive a medal for gallantry. Trompeter was glad to endorse the recommendation and referred it upwards along the chain of command. In time the order came back, dated 10 December 1942, 'in the name of the Fuehrer and the High Command of the Wehrmacht', awarding Fuchs an Iron Cross, Second Class. One can only assume that Trompeter had wilfully failed to inform the High Command that 'Eugen [i.e. Jeno] Fuchs' was a Jew.

This was not quite the end of the affair. Szilagyi records that when General Gustav Jany, the Hungarian commander-in-chief, learned of the award he in turn referred the matter upwards – to Horthy himself. From Horthy the order came back to let the award stand: the Germans were not to be countermanded. And perhaps it gave Horthy some perverse pleasure to think that his overbearing Nazi allies had unknowingly decorated one of 'his' Jews.

In further reward for their efforts Horthy had Fuchs and the rest of his detachment withdrawn from the front and returned home via Vienna. They were not to be called up for front-line labour again, most of them being assigned to war work on the home front while keeping quiet about their Jewish origins.

At this point, Szilagyi's account ends, to be resumed later.

It seems that for the next fifteen months or so Fuchs and his platoon-mates were able to resume their lives in relative safety. Then the Germans invaded, bringing with them Eichmann and his special commando to organize the last mass round-up of the Nazi holocaust. This gives Fuchs the extraordinary distinction of being, surely, the only man in history to be adorned, successively, with an Olympic gold medal, an Iron Cross and a yellow star.

At this point – either out of respect for Fuchs the sportsman, admiration for Fuchs the soldier or compassion for Fuchs the Jew – Almasy comes into the picture. Realizing that Fuchs and his wife and son would be under immediate threat of deportation, he sought them out and sheltered them in a rented suburban house. After some weeks, according to one unverifiable account, he managed to obtain Swedish passports for them and guide them to uncertain sanctuary in one of Wallenberg's safe houses. There, or in hiding elsewhere, they remained until Budapest fell to the advancing Red Army in February 1945.

At least one other Jewish family is known to have been sheltered and fed by Almasy during this period. These were the wife and child of a metalworker named Lajos Weiss who had done some work for Almasy before the war. Weiss was caught in Eichmann's web and deported to Auschwitz, but his wife and son somehow evaded arrest and were given sanctuary by Almasy. As we shall see in a subsequent chapter, the Fuchs and Weiss families both came forward as defence witnesses when Almasy was arraigned as a war criminal before a post-war communist People's Court.

That said, the question remains whether he could or should have done more to help the victims of the Hungarian genocide. Granted, Almasy was no Wallenberg. Unlike Wallenberg, he did not venture out into the streets and the railway stations to confront the Nazis and the Arrow Cross personally and bluff them into turning their captives over to his care. Granted, as a privileged member of the semi-nobility, and a decorated Axis war hero to boot, such daring might not have exposed him to the ultimate risk. Nevertheless, he did act in defiance of the all-powerful Nazis and a rabidly vengeful Arrow Cross regime – and contrary to the cowed acceptance, and in some cases the enthusiastic compliance, of the Hungarian majority. To cite the oft-quoted Talmudic dictum: 'Whoever saves a single soul, it is as if he had saved the whole world.'

All this must at least raise doubts about the allegations that surfaced following publication of Ondaatje's novel and the release of the Hollywood film: that Almasy was a Nazi and by implication a hard-core racist. The irony is that he should have been hounded as a war criminal by the post-war communist regime while his overtly and extravagantly pro-Nazi older brother Janos – close friend if not lover of Unity Mitford and star-struck admirer of Adolf Hitler – would remain unmolested by the Soviets and their Hungarian communist puppets.

Chapter 21

In early February 1945 Budapest fell to the Red Army. In the orgy of rape, looting and indiscriminate arrest that followed, thousands of Hungarian civilians, including Jewish Holocaust survivors and other enemies of the Arrow Cross regime, were hauled off and sent to labour camps in Siberia.

Almasy escaped this fate, if not a worse one, thanks to the Kirghiz minstrel his wayward father had brought home to Borostyanko all those years before. The conversational Russian he had learned from Gyorgy's house guest, and his natural gift for languages, was enough to make him useful to the invaders as an interpreter during the first chaotic weeks of the 'liberation'.

Once the Red Army had got things well enough under control to dispense with his services Almasy travelled west to Burg Bernstein, prudently hoping to avoid the attentions of the puppet regime the Russians had set up to run things in Budapest. At Bernstein he found brother Janos clearing up the mess left behind by the Russians as they passed through on their way westwards to Graz and Vienna. He was surprised and relieved to find that the castle had been spared much of the pillage which had devastated other great houses in the area, such as the Esterhazy family seat in nearby Eisenstadt. Janos was unharmed and feeling rather pleased with himself for having warded off the Russians' depredations so successfully. Their mother Ilona seemed shaken but otherwise in good shape considering her eighty-five years. Janos's crippled wife Princess Maria, forty years Ilona's junior, had weathered the experience less well: a drunken Russian soldier had tried to tip her out of her wheelchair, possibly as a prelude to rape, and had been restrained just in time.

Janos had obviously handled a desperately dangerous situation with a good deal of foresight and common sense, aided by more than a dash of luck. Before the Russians arrived he had hidden away all the castle's easily removable valuables, poured away all the alcohol, including a cellarful of fine wines, and dumped all his firearms into a deep pit in the castle grounds.

His potentially most incriminating possessions – the diaries of Hitler's adoring acolyte Unity Mitford – were most carefully concealed of all. They were political dyna-mite and had they come to the attention of one of the political commissars who accompanied all Soviet military units Janos would have been in trouble. Albeit uneasily, he had kept possession of the diaries – possibly with an eye to their future commercial value – rather than burning them or finding a way of returning them to Unity's family. But his attempts to distance himself from the incriminating diaries without entirely relinquishing them had been some-thing of an exercise in black comedy.

First he had given them for safekeeping to Hannah Mikes (later Van Horne), niece of the Bishop of Szombatheley, fearful that their contents might get him into trouble with the Gestapo. He made Hannah promise not to read the diaries. 'I wish I hadn't kept my word, but I did [keep her word],' as she later recalled. 'After some months he took them back.'

Sensing that the heat was off so far as the Nazis were concerned, Janos kept the diaries at Burg Bernstein for the next two or three years but then, as the war began to go badly for the Germans, he became nervous about them again and begged Laszlo to hide them in the family mansion on Miklos Horthy Avenue. During that period, Laszlo's niece Zita (later Baroness Stoerck) stayed in Laszlo's flat and stole a look at the diaries. They contained 'a regular timetable – what she was doing, whom she met: Goebbels was there, Hitler was wonderful, she was thrilled, that kind of thing', she would recall later. 'Horrible platitudes. I read them and could hardly believe it was possible. To have been there and to have taken in so little!'

As the tide of war in the east began to turn decisively Laszlo decided to send the diaries back to Burg Bernstein and Zita volunteered to take them there in person – half a dozen volumes bound in black cloth, together with albums of press cuttings and signed photographs of Hitler, which she packed into a rucksack. 'Janos was half crying with fear when he saw them,' Zita would recall. 'But they were hidden in Bernstein, until a few years later a Dutch priest, Father Koster, took them to Lady Redesdale.'

The Red Army occupied Bernstein and its castle on Easter Sunday, 1 April 1945. Janos has left a detailed written account of what happened. This obviously self-serving document, compiled by Janos some years later, was found in a desk drawer at Burg Bernstein following his death in 1975. It may not be entirely truthful but is interesting enough to quote at some length:

. . . One had to try to save the castle [he wrote] . . . to have run away would have been unforgiveable. Silver, linen, etc. was hidden in the roof. Shotguns buried outside the house. Wine and spirits poured away, even cider, though I poured the cider away later after a Russian had drunk 12 litres and become insensible . . .

All drawers in the house should be left open and unlocked . . . I myself forgot the writing table in the back drawing room, which was promptly broken into. On March 30 I threw captured Russian weapons and my army pistols from the first world war into the *Tiefen Brunnen* (deep well) . . . if the Russians had found them they would have shot me . . . All the photographs of people in Nazi uniform I burned, as did my wife also. She kept just one. The Russians found it and I was very nearly shot as a result . . . The picture showed me and Pal Drascovic both in civilian clothes surrounded by SA [Nazi stormtroopers] at the opening ceremony of the *Finanzburo* in Gussing in 1938.

In the last few days before the arrival of the Russians, small units of the retreating Wehrmacht passed through Bernstein, including air force personnel from a nearby base, one of whom was the nephew of Reichsmarschall Hermann Goering. 'He was quite certain that his uncle would play a great part in the [post-war] reconstruction of Germany and was hurt that I disagreed.' Small units of the Hungarian Army passed the same way, 'cursing and blaming each other;

they had completely lost their heads'. There were relatively few civilian refugees, and these travelling mostly in horse-drawn carts. 'They begged to stay here overnight and asked for food and milk for their children. One did what one could; it was often heartbreaking . . . They all had terrible atrocity stories.'

As Easter Sunday – and the Red Army – drew ever closer, Janos prepared a number of coloured eggs: 'I had made a plan.'

The first of April dawned quietly. The stream of refugees had dried up. The silence was punctuated by the sound of distant gunfire and Allied bombing attacks on the German air base at Wienerneustadt. The weather was warm, the day beautiful. 'Our peacocks proudly displayed and strutted, a very peaceful sight.'

At about 5 p.m., noticing an unusual white object between the trees on the approach to the castle, Janos took a closer look through his field glasses. The object turned out to be the fur hat of a Russian scout, evidently observing the castle to ascertain whether it was defended. 'The attack would take two or three hours, so one might expect it tomorrow,' Janos predicted. 'Why should they bother to risk a night attack? They had plenty of time. I did not sleep very well that night.'

I got up very early and went down to the office . . . Behind the office stood the police commandant, Meister Anhalt. He was dressed up like a Christmas tree – long coat, steel helmet on his head, gas mask about his neck, gun in his hand, swords and truncheon hanging from his belt, also knuckledusters and handcuffs. A large bag hung from him as well; he could hardly move. I asked him 'What are you doing?' The answer came uneasily, 'I am holding the line.' 'Well, get on with holding it,' I replied . . .

From his observation point by the swimming pool, Janos saw the Russians swarming down the hillside towards the castle. There was sporadic shooting which soon diminished as the Russians realized there was no opposition. After a while Janos saw a Russian soldier 'picking his way quite happily through the vegetable garden. He carried a [sub-machine-] gun under one arm and was playing a mouth organ.'

At this point Janos and his head gamekeeper, Michael Furst, ran back to the castle, stopping off to look into the chapel where the curate Ecker was kneeling in prayer. 'You stay where you are. The Russians are coming,' Janos shouted.

Inside the castle, Janos had servants carry his wife to join his mother in her ground-floor *Gottgetrost* suite.

The courtyard filled with soldiers and occasional shots rang out. I went out slowly with my arms up and called out loudly '*Zvdravstvuitje*' good morning . . . A Russian walked up to me and asked '*Skoliko tschas?*' – what's the time? I looked at my watch and before I could blink he had whipped it off and put it on, giving me his in exchange, which did not work properly. I was wearing a Styrian hunting jacket. One of them tore at the shoulder tab and shouted 'soldier!' I shook my head. '*Niet, ochotnjik*' – no, huntsman. I can no longer remember accurately and in what order things happened. Everyone looked after themselves . . . Sometimes shots rang out and sometimes I heard

German flak. We were caught in cross-fire from Mariasdorf. Fortunately they were shooting high . . .

In the kitchen Janos found the maid Maria working to feed a group of Russian soldiers. Janos gave one of them, a heavily bemedalled veteran, one of the painted Easter eggs he had prepared in advance, saying in Russian: 'Christ is risen.' To which the answer might have been a bullet had the Red Army veteran been as dedicated a communist as Janos had until recently been a fanatical pro-Nazi. But it was a well-calculated risk; the old soldier gave the traditional answer 'Christ is risen, indeed' and accepted the egg. Encouraged, and no doubt greatly relieved, Janos pressed home his advantage.

I handed out Easter eggs indiscriminately and they all answered the greeting. An approving murmur followed. The decorated soldier patted me on the shoulder: 'You are a good man. Are you the mayor?'

But the danger was far from past. When Red Army soldiers wanted to make off with a car which the local doctor had left parked in the castle forecourt, they demanded the ignition key from Janos. His protestations that the car was not his and that the key was in the doctor's room in the village 'did not help at all'.

An unpleasant young chap with silver crowned teeth . . . got me by the collar and dragged me out cursing. At the lower gate he kicked me up the arse. I stumbled . . . he raised his rifle to his shoulder and pointed it at me. I screamed with the strength of the desperate, *Blagodarsu vas*. This worked . . . he let me get up and we went down to the doctor's house and searched . . . I only understood later why the boy had laughed at me: I had muddled my Russian and had thanked him for shooting at me.

Back at the castle the Russians had begun full-scale looting, breaking into boxes with axes looking for valuables and money. 'On the stairs, in the passages, the Russians were swarming. Every cupboard and drawer was open and they searched everything but appeared only interested in clothes. They stepped out of their trousers and chucked them into the alpine garden in the courtyard. They changed their shirts but not their jackets and boots.'

Then Janos heard an outcry from the *Gottgetrost* suite where a Russian was trying to tip Princess Maria out of her wheelchair.

My mother was calling for help. The Russian struck her in the breast, but he did leave Maria alone. An officer came along and threw the soldier out. [He] then came to me in the kitchen and asked if I wished to have the soldier shot.

During that confused and chaotic day there was one incident which, in Janos's telling, seems almost dream-like.

Suddenly two horsemen rode into the courtyard . . . One of them was wearing a red-brown Tartar smock with stitched bullet pockets . . . On his head he had a tall fur cap and his manly, beautiful face, with a proud eagle nose, was burned quite brown. His arms were also genuine Tartar and very beautiful. He carried a silver shield and a superb sabre hung at his saddle. In one hand he held a whip and in the other a map. Reins were loose over the neck of an exquisite, well-groomed horse. I did not notice that he had any firearms. He was like an apparition from the time of Gehamyla. His companion, on almost as lovely a horse, also appeared to be without [fire]arms. I gawked at them with my mouth wide open . . .

By nightfall the castle was completely empty of the Russians. They had moved on to the west and the ordeal was over. Janos was 'astounded that such troops were so disciplined, but I found out later that they were terrified of the enormous, forbidding castle'.

Although Janos's past history (and future behaviour) does not suggest a man in whom one would repose great trust, his account of that day's almost surreal happenings does somehow ring true – and, given his extremist right-wing views and the Russian 'liberators'' general reputation for violence and brutality – surprisingly fair-minded. What also comes across strongly is the indifference and sparsity of Janos's references to his crippled wife. She died two years later, aged only forty-seven. After a decent interval Janos married Baroness Pacetta Kufstein.

Chapter 22

Not long after his return to his birthplace Laszlo found himself again in the hands of the Russians, not this time as an interpreter but as a prisoner of the NKVD secret police, who sent him back to Budapest for interrogation. He had been denounced as a 'class enemy', a Nazi sympathizer and a war criminal.

His lengthy and brutal interrogation was conducted at 60 Andrassy Boulevard, the former headquarters of the Arrow Cross police and future headquarters of their seamless Hungarian communist successors, the AVO. As during the Nazi occupation, the home-grown secret police had nothing to learn from their foreign role models in sadism and the application of terror.*

Laszlo spent eight months under questioning by the NKVD and their AVO acolytes at Andrassy Boulevard before appearing in front of a People's Court for trial, conviction and sentence, a sequence that was invariably a matter of routine. If he has left an account of his sufferings under interrogation it has not yet surfaced; suffice it to say that he weighed a modest 154 pounds (70 kg.) when he

---

* 60 Andrassy Boulevard with its gruesome contents was opened to the public in February 2001, as the 'House of Terror Museum'. One exhibit – a printed instruction to prison guards – embodies the ethos of this dreadful place: 'Don't just guard, hate.'

went into custody and a skeletal 90 pounds (40 kg.) when he came out. Nevertheless, in his written confession as presented to the court, he seems to have conceded little.

Yes, he had performed intelligence functions for the Germans. Yes, as a Hungarian he had volunteered for secondment to the Wehrmacht and had been awarded two medals for his services. Yes, he was the author of *With Rommel's Army in Libya* and had lived on its earnings. Yes, he had believed in a German victory and, although having left the Abwehr through ill health, had been in contact with Nazi occupation officials and leading Hungarian fascists in 1944. But no, he had given them no information; no, he was not anti-semitic; and no, he was never a member of the Arrow Cross.

There was little here for a conviction, even by the elastic standards of a People's Court, so the prosecution cited *With Rommel's Army in Libya* – an innocuous enough text, to be sure, whose worst offence apparently was to contain one or two admiring references to Field Marshal Rommel* – as evidence of his crimes against the Hungarian people. Even that evidential scrap might have been enough to consign Almasy either to a long spell in prison, or even to a death sentence (he was, after all, a 'class enemy' and four hundred of those were to be sent to the gallows by the People's Courts), but for an intervention from an entirely unlikely source: the hard-line Hungarian Communist Party leader, Matyas Rakosi.

* Winston Churchill himself had done no less during a House of Commons debate, calling Rommel 'a very daring and skilful opponent . . . and, may I say across the havoc of war, a great general'.

Rakosi had spent the war years in Moscow and had returned to Budapest with the Red Army as Stalin's hand-picked man to become puppet ruler of post-war Hungary. He knew nothing about the Almasy case – one of a large number pending before the new regime's People's Courts – and cared even less. But he had fond memories of his student years before World War I at Budapest's Eastern Academy, where his tutor was the celebrated Orientalist, Professor Gyula Germanus.* And Germanus, as it happened, owed a huge debt of gratitude to Almasy.

In 1930, while on a field trip into the Libyan Desert, Germanus's unaccompanied vehicle had broken down. Stranded, and with a limited supply of water, he might well have perished but for the providential appearance on the scene of Almasy, who fixed his vehicle and escorted him to safety. Germanus did not forget and when, sixteen years later, he heard that Almasy was in custody and facing trial as a war criminal, he offered himself as a defence witness.

The court president, Dr Ivan Lukacs, unwilling to permit any interference with the rough justice he intended to administer, declined to admit Germanus's testimony. And there the matter might have ended, with Almasy's inevitable conviction, but for the old connection between Stalin's pro-consul and his former tutor.

Germanus encountered no difficulty in obtaining an appointment with Rakosi. His name was enough to dismantle the inevitable bureaucratic barriers between the

* Born Jewish, Germanus converted to Islam during his twenties. Unlike many converted Jews, his privileged status allowed him to avoid deportation during the Holocaust. He lived on until 1979.

communist boss and a petitioner. Sitting in Rakosi's office Germanus explained his special interest in the Almasy case and complained of the court's refusal to hear his testimony. With almost no further discussion, Rakosi picked up the telephone, called Lukacs and told him he wanted Germanus to be admitted as a witness. Lukacs needed no further explanation. So far as he was concerned, the boss was instructing him in barely disguised code that Almasy had to be set free. When the case came to court on 16 November, the proceedings were brief. Without mentioning the desert rescue, Germanus testified that he could detect no special pro-German bias in Almasy's book on the war in North Africa, although his praise for Rommel's generalship might be 'a matter of debate'. He, Germanus, had met a British officer in Budapest who had inquired about Almasy because 'he wanted to meet a brave colleague'.

Germanus did perhaps overstate the case by adding, apparently gratuitously, that Almasy's entire family were anti-fascist and had even been harassed by the Arrow Cross. This was certainly questionable, but nothing Germanus had to say would have been questioned.

The next defence witness was the Jewish metalworker, Lajos Weiss, not long back from Auschwitz. He said he had known Almasy since 1937 and had 'done a lot of work for him'. When he was deported to Poland by the Nazis, Almasy had sheltered and fed his family 'for free, out of humanity'.

On the opposing side three hostile witnesses were listed – Dr Arpadna Kartal and his wife Agnes, who deposed that Almasy was a right-winger whose flat contained only right-wing books, and Zoltan Racz, who would testify that Almasy was an outright fascist. All three may be considered to have had a stake in Almasy's conviction. The communist authorities had allocated them apartments in the Almasy mansion and, in fact, the Kartals were living in Laszlo's ground-floor flat.

For the defence, Jeno Fuchs's wife and son were waiting to testify – but not Fuchs himself. The reason for his absence from the witness list was the Iron Cross which, according to Szilagyi's detailed account, he had won on the Eastern Front. The former Olympic champion was himself serving a sentence in the notorious Pestvideki Prison as a fascist sympathizer and under the circumstances it might have seemed inappropriate for Dr Lukacs to call the wife and son of one war criminal to give evidence in the defence of another.

So the testimony of the Fuchs family – presumably telling how Almasy had sheltered and fed them: for why else would they have risked coming forward for the defence? – went unheard and unfortunately remains unheard and, in any detail, unknown to this day.

At this point in Almasy's trial it remained only for Lukacs to order an adjournment so that the prosecution could go through the motions of searching Almasy's book for the 'guilty' passages. And here was another scene of black comedy: when the court reassembled on 23 November, the Prosecutor, Pal Kadar, had to admit that he had been unable to find the book. All copies had been destroyed by order of the occupation authorities.* At this, Judge Lukacs lost no time in announcing: 'This case is dropped accordingly. The accused is to be released immediately.'

As for the driven, conflicted, heroic, tragic – and ultimately pathetic – Jeno Fuchs, he remained in jail until he died, aged seventy-three, on 14 March 1955. He wanted above all to be considered an unhyphenated Hungarian and would go to extraordinary lengths to stake his claim; but he would not, or could not, deny that he was a Jew. As a consequence of his Iron Cross he was allowed to be neither a true Hungarian nor a proper Jew. A non-person to the post-war remnants of the Jewish community, as to Hungarian society at large, his extraordinary history is nowadays unknown to the majority and covered up by the few who do know it.

Almasy's respite from the attentions of the communists was brief. A formal acquittal by a local People's Court meant little to the NKVD, who answered only to the Kremlin, and within two months he was back in the interrogation centre on Andrassy Boulevard, this time being questioned about his suspected links with Western intelligence.

The details of such alleged activities are no doubt mouldering away in locked KGB and MI6 files on both sides of

---

* One lone copy of the book was found more than half a century later in, of all places, the US Library of Congress in Washington, DC. It was translated into English by Gabriel Francis Horchler and republished in 1999 (see Bibliography) with an introduction by Dr Kubassek.

what used to be called the Iron Curtain. But there is persuasive anecdotal evidence (from sources that cannot be cited) that Almasy had been operating a clandestine radio in Budapest, giving Britain's MI6 political intelligence and information about Soviet military movements.

What we know with more certainty is that at some time during Almasy's detention and interrogation over the next six months – and most probably at British instigation – Alaeddin Moukhtar, a cousin of King Farouk and a senior official of the Egyptian court, delivered a substantial bribe to Almasy's Hungarian jailers to connive at his 'escape'.

The bribe was taken, although the how, where and when of Almasy's escape remain undisclosed. Once free, and travelling under false papers as Josef Grossmann, a gaunt, wasted Almasy made his way to the British zone of tripartite Vienna and thence to Trieste, where the United Kingdom consulate had been forewarned to expect him. There, Almasy was provided with British travel documents, a rail ticket to Rome, an air ticket from Rome to Cairo (for where else would Almasy, homeless and hounded, want to go but back to the desert he loved?) and a small amount of pocket money.

Some uncertainty may remain about whether or not Almasy had become a double agent simultaneously serving the Abwehr and the British towards the end of World War II, but there can be little doubt that by 1945–6 he was a Cold War asset for British intelligence. If not, they would scarcely have gone to such lengths to extricate him from Hungary and the clutches of the NKVD. Nor would the NKVD have gone to equal lengths to recapture him.

By the time Almasy crossed the frontier into Allied-occupied Italy, they were hot on his trail.

Chapter 23

If Jean Howard, the Bletchley Park intelligence analyst who set the alarm bells ringing for Almasy in 1942, is pure le Carré, her old friend and post-war MI6 colleague Ronnie Valderano seems more in the vein of Ian Fleming's Agent 007.

At the age of eighty-five, Valderano retains vestiges of a poised and stylish younger self when, according to his memoirs, he travelled the world about the business of Her Majesty's Secret Service accompanied by his equally poised and stylish, crack shot wife, Honor. It was Valderano who was given the task of spiriting Almasy to safety out of Allied-occupied Italy, an assignment he seems to have performed with brio.

Born Ronald Waring in 1918, he had been a World War II officer in the British Army and by 1947 was working for the Secret Intelligence Service (MI6) in Rome with the rank of colonel and under the cover of a bogus import–export company named Tarlair. Somehow and somewhere along the line since then, Colonel Waring has acquired a rather more elevated persona, styling himself 'His Grace the 18th Duke of Valderano' and laying claim to a lineage so thoroughly lost in the mists of antiquity that even the internet's principal genealogy websites (and the old-fashioned reference books of the European aristocracy, such as the venerable *Almanach de Gotha*) cannot seem to find either the name or the title. '*Nessun risultato* – No matches were found' is the websites' invariable response to a search request.

Waring/Valderano sports a number of additional titles – subsidiary but no less archaic-exotic than his dukedom: Marquess of Rio Castel, Count of Varinge, Hereditary Knight of the Sword Belt, Knight Grand Cross of the Order of St Ignatius of Antioch, and so forth.

And if this display of blood indigo and his recollections of action and adventure fail to impress, he has other claims to singularity. He recalls in his memoirs that as a student in pre-war Germany he was invited to tea at Berchtesgaden, where he met not only Hitler but also Goering, Goebbels and the Nazi Finance Minister Hjalmar Schacht. One might imagine he had gate-crashed a Nazi cabinet meeting.

But there is more; 'I knew Mussolini well. He used to come up for luncheon at my mother's villa near Rome. Later I was to meet [the Spanish dictator] Franco, [the Portuguese dictator] Salazar, De Gaulle, Eisenhower and Churchill.' Full house? Not quite: 'I was also for a short time a stand-in ADC to Field Marshal Montgomery and I had luncheon with Pope John Paul II when he was a simple priest in Rome.'

Waring/Valderano was born towards the end of World War I, the son of a Captain H. Waring, who gave his address as the Cavalry Club, Piccadilly. He was put down at birth for Eton but his father sent him instead to the less venerable but no less elitist Stowe School in Buckinghamshire. After two years there, as a resident of Chandos House, young

Ronald had to be taken out following a contretemps between his father and his housemaster. He seems to have completed his education in France and Germany and by the outbreak of World War II he was an officer in the Royal Hampshire Regiment, eventually seeing active service with the 8th Army in the 1943–5 Italian campaign. During this time he claims to have been a liaison officer between the British military and the anti-fascist Italian partisans.

Whatever the reality of his claim to an unlisted Italian dukedom, it must be allowed that Waring/Valderano does project an impressively grand ducal style. But can his account of rescuing Almasy from the clutches of the NKVD and seeing him safely off to Egypt be considered any more authentic than his title?

In support of his veracity in this matter, it should be borne in mind that for a secret agent, active or retired, personal identity is a somewhat elastic concept. The acquisition of a cover name and a pseudo-identity goes, as they say, with the territory. And in any event, for quite a number of Italians, whatever their occupation, a claim to nobility is a mere commonplace. As that unblinking observer of his countrymen's foibles, Luigi Barzini, has noted: 'Today, many nobles in Italy are as phony as stage jewellery . . . It is roughly calculated that the Italian Republic can boast ten times as many nobles as there were under the Monarchy.' If the Italian-Englishman Ronald Waring has taken a cue from his quasi-compatriots who is to blame him? And if his espionage background is one in which assumed identity is a matter of stock-in-trade who should be surprised?

So his claims to an ancient dukedom and to nodding

acquaintanceship with a quiverful of European dictators do not necessarily cast doubts on his veracity about operational matters. Almost by definition, the details of undercover intelligence operations must remain officially unacknowledged and publicly undocumented. Usually we only have the participants' word for what happened, should the Official Secrets Act allow them to talk at all. And in the case of Almasy's escape from the NKVD, all but one of the participants is dead.

That said, Waring/Valderano's account, as given in his (privately published) memoirs and in an interview he gave to Almasy's Hungarian biographer, Dr Kubassek, rings true enough, even though it does read in places like paperback spy fiction. Inevitably, perhaps, there are minor discrepancies between the account Waring/Valderano wrote for his memoirs and the account he gave in his interview with Kubassek. But in essentials the two versions tally. The following is a conflation of the two.

The episode began when Waring/Valderano received a message from his MI6 controller in late August or early September of 1947, telling him to pick up Almasy from a certain small hotel in Rome's Via Nazionale and get him on the first available flight to Cairo. It continued with a further signal warning that the NKVD were already hot on Almasy's trail. When they met, Waring/Valderano found his man in 'very bad physical and psychological condition'.

[He] looked like a living skeleton covered by skin. He was tall and thin but seemed as if he had no flesh or muscles . . . He also behaved very strangely. He often shuddered at anything and turned his head left and right. Sometimes he looked behind as if he were afraid of someone. And he trembled all over. He spoke slowly in a drawling voice and he stuttered, although his English was excellent . . . His hand shook when he lit a cigarette – he was a heavy smoker – and sometimes his body jerked, too, and his shoulders twitched.

Almasy knew that the NKVD had picked up his trail in Trieste. They had been unable to seize him on the train from Trieste to Rome. It was crowded with potential witnesses and, with Italy still under Allied occupation, the British and US military police were liable to make spot checks of railway passengers.

Leaving the train at Rome, Almasy gave his pursuers the slip and went by taxi to the designated hotel in the Via Nazionale where he left his hand luggage containing his passport, plane ticket and a few personal items with the receptionist before telephoning Waring/Valderano as instructed. The British agent sent his Hungarian assistant Deszo de Onody – formerly secretary to Admiral Horthy's son, Miklos junior, and personally known to Almasy – to pick him up and take him to Waring/Valderano's house in the Via Donizetti.

Within minutes of Almasy and Onody leaving the hotel two men arrived, wearing long dark coats and hats in defiance of the summer heat. From the cut of their un-seasonable clothes they were clearly from the east. They hung around the hotel entrance but did not go inside, apparently waiting for Almasy to turn up. Almasy's flight to Cairo was not scheduled to take off until five the following morning from Ciampino airport, but Waring/ Valderano decided it was not safe for him to return to the hotel. He would keep Almasy for the night and drive him to Ciampino in his powerful, hand-built Allard touring car. But on the way they must call into Almasy's hotel to collect his hand luggage and travel documents from the reception desk.

We set out at four in the morning [he told Kubassek]. I was accompanied by my wife, who was also an officer and an excellent target shooter, Onody and Almasy. We all had guns except Almasy. I drove the Allard. We stopped in a small street near the Via Nazionale. We switched off the lights but not the engine. My wife, who looked Italian and spoke the language fluently, walked to the hotel.

The night porter was half-asleep. Waring/Valderano's wife asked for the key to Almasy's room and the bag he had left behind the desk. The somnolent night porter handed them over and the lady walked calmly not to the lift but to the exit. Once in the street she hurried to the waiting car.

The two NKVD men who had been lurking in the shadows outside realized something was up and hurried after her. She reached the Allard well ahead of them and Waring/Valderano sped away. The two Russians followed in their own car which, lacking the high-powered Allard's acceleration and turn of speed, fell far behind.

Scorching through the semi-deserted streets of the sleeping Italian capital, Waring/Valderano stopped at an Allied military checkpoint on the approaches to the airport. He showed his pass and instructed the guards to stop any car that might be following.

When they got to Ciampino the Cairo flight was already on the runway, taxiing for take-off. Waring/Valderano again showed his pass to get through a checkpoint at the perimeter fence and drove in front of the taxiing plane, forcing it to stop. The pilot was not at all pleased at this intervention and some hard words were exchanged before he agreed to lower a rope ladder and take Almasy aboard.

Almasy was so weak he couldn't climb the rope ladder. He had to be drawn up to the plane. We pushed him from below while the crew pulled and lifted him into the plane. This is how Almasy got out of Rome.

Can we believe Waring/Valderano's account? In essentials, yes. The Egyptian bribe to the Hungarian secret police; Almasy's subsequent flight from Soviet-occupied Hungary into Austria; his acquisition of a false passport in Vienna and of further false ID – plus rail and air tickets – in Trieste; none of this could have been accomplished without the active intervention of British intelligence. And British intelligence would surely not have gone to such lengths for anyone but an 'asset' to whom they owed a great deal. Nor could Almasy have got from Rome to Cairo without more of the same kind of assistance. Waring/Valderano's account, enhanced though it may be in some details, seems to be the only rational explanation of how Almasy got away.

Chapter 24

On Almasy's arrival in Cairo, Moukhtar and a British intelligence agent were waiting for him. After clearing the formalities, they set him up in a small flat in the fashionable Zamalek district of central Cairo. From that point his usefulness to MI6 seems to have ended, although Moukhtar remained a faithful friend in court.

As he slowly recovered his strength Almasy began to earn a meagre living, as before, as a flight instructor at Almaza airport. Poverty and ill health had not quenched his thirst for adventure. Between giving flying lessons to wealthy young Egyptians he led desert expeditions for rich Americans. In 1948 he turned his back on the desert for a while to lead a hunting safari to Mozambique. Later that year he established some kind of a record by towing a glider from Paris to Cairo, making only two stops en route.

But all the time he remained obsessed by the prospect of finding the legendary lost army of Cambyses. 'He had no money at all, but he always had lots of plans,' recalls Waring/Valderano, who renewed his acquaintanceship with Almasy in 1949 when Laszlo was staying with a wartime Abwehr colleague in Austria.

Almasy's post-war life seemed to be going nowhere when, in 1950, his long-held ambition suddenly came to fruition. Partly as a gesture of piety towards the memory of his father – and apparently unaware that Fuad had turned down Almasy's proposal in 1936 – the playboy King Farouk decided to go ahead and launch the Cairo Desert Institute with Almasy as its director. His motive, as already noted, was at least in part to cock a thinly disguised public snook at the British. And though it must have seemed unlikely at the time, neither the British nor Farouk had long left to lord it over the Egyptians.

The opening of the Desert Institute was Almasy's moment of supreme triumph, but his health – undermined by years of desert hardship and months of ill-treatment at the hands of the Soviet and Hungarian secret police, and given the limitations of medicine and pharmacology at the time – was failing beyond hope of recovery. A photograph of the time, probably the last ever taken of him, shows a scarcely recognizable, balding figure, improbably playing an accordion.

Within a couple of weeks of Farouk's grand party at the Abdin Palace, Almasy experienced a sudden back pain under the right ribs and collapsed. He was diagnosed as suffering from severe hepatitis complicated by an attack of amoebic dysentery. From a Cairo hospital he was flown at royal expense first to Innsbruck and thence on to a private clinic in Salzburg run by a Dr Viktor Wehrle, who immediately administered a massive blood transfusion. Almasy was running a temperature of 104°F (39°C) and an X-ray revealed that he had a seriously abscessed liver. Doctor Wehrle operated the next day and found a huge multi-cellular abscess. He gave his patient several more blood transfusions and injections of the new antibiotic, penicillin.

But there was no hope. In his semi-comatose condition Almasy babbled about Cambyses and the lost army. According to Jean Howard, he had no visitors. At three in the afternoon of 22 March 1951, he died.

The day of his funeral was very cold. A horse-drawn hearse carried him to his grave site (Parcel 75, Row 4, Number 2) in Salzburg's municipal cemetery. There were only two wreaths and the only mourners present were Laszlo's doctor and a priest, his brother Janos and Janos's second wife, Baroness Kufstein. Laszlo's mother, the ill-used Ilona Pittoni, was still alive but too frail to attend.

Shortly after Laszlo's funeral Janos went to Cairo to dispose of his effects. In the flat at Zamalek he found virtually nothing apart from a few sticks of furniture – no notes, no letters, no diaries, no maps and no money. The place had been cleaned out, either by Almasy's house servant, who was missing, or more credibly by British and/or Egyptian intelligence.

The Salzburg municipal cemetery is seriously over-crowded. One may rent grave space in it on a renewable twenty-year lease. Janos paid for the first twenty years. When he died in 1971 he made no provision in his will for a renewal and the grave was 'sold' again. On 31 January 1973, a coffin containing the body of a woman named Amalia Deutscher was interred on top of Almasy's.

Yet another twenty years on – by which time Almasy had achieved posthumous if somewhat spurious fame as 'the English Patient' – the lease on the grave ran out yet again. This time a group of admirers organized by a Hungarian National Airlines pilot named Josef Kasza raised the money to prevent Almasy's burial site being invaded a second time and obtained permission to erect a memorial plaque on the site. At about the same time, Dr Kubassek, as director of Hungary's National Geographical Museum at Erd, near Budapest, commissioned a bronze bust of Almasy and installed it, alongside those of other notable Hungarian explorers, in the museum's grounds. A modest memorial plaque also adorns the arch through which one enters the courtyard of Almasy's birthplace, Burg Bernstein. It records that the Bedouin had dubbed him Abu Ramleh, Father of the Dunes.

It might more memorably and appropriately have quoted the valedictory passage from his introduction to *The Unknown Sahara*:

In the infinity of the desert body and mind are cleansed. Man feels nearer to the Creator, from whom nothing any longer diverts his attention. Almost invisibly an unshakeable belief in a mighty Power above us brings resignation to our humble human existence, even to the extent of offering our life to the desert without a grudge.

Postscript

It is better to travel hopefully than to arrive.
Robert Louis Stevenson

In my search for the real English Patient I have travelled
both hopefully and sceptically. Readers may feel that I have
not fully arrived – although that may not be so important.
As Stevenson suggested, the journey itself is the reward.

So, have all the questions been answered? Was Almasy
an Axis spy and were his pre-war desert expeditions a cover
for espionage? Was it conviction or opportunism that sent
him back to North Africa for the Abwehr during World
War II? Was it compassion for the persecuted or indignation
at the Nazi occupation of Hungary that drove him to
become a double agent and shelter a handful of Jews during
the Holocaust? And so forth . . .

If 'to arrive' is to reach firm conclusions about any or all
of the above, I must admit that no, I have not. The evidence
has been contradictory and confusing, the sand constantly
shifting, and Almasy remains an enigma to the last. Which
is perhaps as it should be.

One thing that is not in doubt is that, for all his occasional
embellishments and exaggerations, Almasy's achievements
as an explorer and pioneer of motorized desert travel are

considerable. As Rupert Harding–Newman told me: 'I only met him once and that was in the Sudan in the early thirties. I had been reassigned from the LRDG by the time he turned up, working for the Germans during the war, and I have no opinions about that. But there's no doubt, he knew a lot about the desert.' That last was scarcely an overstatement.

Another thing about Almasy that should be given due weight is that there is nothing in his published writings that even hints at a belief in Nazi ideology or that he was tainted by the rabid judophobia of his brother Janos and the lunatic occultism they were exposed to at Burg Bernstein in their youth. So far as I have been able to ascertain, none of those who knew Almasy personally thought he was pro-Nazi.

'If he had any affiliations with the Nazis it was never more than a casual matter,' said his Cairo socialite friend Victor-Mansour Semeika. 'This may have had its origins when his brother and Adolf Hitler were being simultaneously courted by . . . Unity Mitford.' Peter Clayton concurred: 'My mother couldn't stand him and my father knew he was a homosexual, but he never thought he was a Nazi.' And even Bill Kennedy Shaw, who had little time for Almasy either, thought he was no more than an old-fashioned royalist, albeit with authoritarian inclinations.

Regarding Almasy's wartime service in North Africa, it should be stressed that the desert war was a relatively gentlemanly affair, with both sides observing the Geneva Convention and virtually no civilian population on hand to get caught in the crossfire.

As Rommel himself said, it was war without hate and as a participant in that war Almasy was unlikely to have done anything that could be classed as criminal. Nor was working for the Abwehr in any way comparable to working for the Gestapo or the SS. On the whole, it was straightforward intelligence work without the disfiguring element of brutality and sadism.

As for the relatively minor yet quite extraordinary subplot concerning the Olympic medallist Jeno Fuchs and his Iron Cross, this took a good deal of tracking down and seems likely to arouse a good deal of controversy. All attempts to secure confirmation of the story from the Jewish community in Budapest met with a blank response, denoting either disbelief or embarrassed silence. There was a similar reaction from Hungarian gentiles who might be in a position to know.

Joseph (Tommy) Lapid, a Hungarian Holocaust survivor and currently Deputy Prime Minister of Israel, said in answer to my queries that he found the story 'unbelievable and even absurd'. Doctor Kubassek, Almasy's (non-Jewish) biographer, was apparently quite unaware of the story and also found it barely credible. Dezso Vad, in charge of the Hungarian Olympic Committee's official publications, was noticeably uncooperative when asked for further details.

Yet, strange though the tale may be, the detailed circumstantial information provided by Gyorgy Szilagyi* –

---

* Gyorgy Szilagyi is a common Hungarian name and without Mr Vad's cooperation it proved impossible to contact him for further information.

and the confirmation by two Hungarian lexicons – that Fuchs was awarded the German medal seems quite compelling. So is the incontrovertible fact of Fuchs's post-war imprisonment on war crimes charges.

I had never heard of Laszlo Almasy until I read *The English Patient* ten years ago and even then did not realize that its protagonist was based on a non-fictional character. But his gaunt ghost has been shadowing me, unbidden and intermittently, ever since.

It was only after I had read the novel (with some admiration) and seen the film that I discovered there really had been a Laszlo Almasy. I came across a reference to him while researching, with co-author Colin Smith, for *Fire in the Night*, a biography of Orde Wingate. Almasy's name popped up again in 1999 while I was again researching with Colin for *Alamein*, our account of the 1940–43 North African campaign.

When, following publication of *Alamein*, it was suggested that I write a biography of Almasy, I had mixed feelings. I was not at all sure that I wanted to put my name to a book that might appear to be less a genuine biography than a ride on the coat-tails of *The English Patient*; I was not at all sure that Almasy was interesting enough a character to bear the weight of a full treatment; I was not at all sure that if I delved deep enough I wouldn't find something nasty in the woodshed (remember, 'a Nazi but a sportsman' had been the verdict of the *Geographical Journal*); and I was not at all sure that, being ignorant of the fiendishly difficult Hungarian language, I could unearth and make sense of enough primary source material to justify a biography.

In the event, I went ahead with the project, but the problem of source documents remained. As I was soon to discover, the originals of many of these had been given to the former MI6 agent Jean Howard by Almasy's niece, his only surviving relative.

The papers had been handed over in 1995 when Mrs Howard, Waring/Valderano, Peter Clayton and two anonymous but apparently senior ex-MI6 men went to Burg Bernstein to commemorate Almasy's one hundredth birth date. Kurt Mayer, who was on hand to film the occasion for a TV documentary, found the candle-lit celebration dinner in the *Rittersaal* somewhat bizarre. Peter Clayton, who had been invited as the only one, apart from Waring/Valerano, to have actually met Almasy – and who had brought along his father's photographs of their joint expeditions – thought the entire event, beginning at Heathrow, was 'worth a guinea a minute'.

Jean Howard was intent on writing her own Almasy biography, and when I met her for the first time in the summer of 2002 she declined my suggestion that we collaborate. I had no hard feelings: Mrs Howard is a remarkable and formidable lady and I wished her every success before setting off to look for the essential source material elsewhere. In this I have been lucky in getting a great deal of spontaneous help from a number of people.

Doctor Janos Kubassek, director of the Hungarian National Geographic Museum at Erd, had tirelessly and assiduously hunted down every scrap of documentation relating to the early life of Almasy, for whom he has the greatest admiration. When I approached him, rather hesitantly seeking guidance, Dr Kubassek generously allowed me to make what use I wished of material published in his own Almasy biography, *A Szahara Buvoleteben* (for publishing details see Bibliography).

Grateful as I am for that, I feel bound to say in fairness to Dr Kubassek that he and I must disagree on the subject of Almasy's sex life. Kubassek insists most emphatically that Almasy was not a homosexual and says he has found evidence of his relationship with two women. If so, that does not exclude the possibility that Almasy was, if not exclusively homosexual, then at the very least bisexual. To dwell on this subject is not prurient: it is surely necessary for an understanding of Almasy's elusive persona. It should also be borne in mind that, even in today's open climate, homosexuality remains a taboo subject in Hungary.

I'm very much indebted, too, to Andras Zboray for his invaluable English translation of *Az Ismeretlen Szahara* (*The Unknown Sahara*), Almasy's 1934 account of his early desert travels. It provides a more immediate and authentic account than Almasy's revised 1939 German translation of the same work, *Unbekannte Sahara*, which omits some material, adds some, and is less candid on certain points. Zboray's translation is available on the internet via www.fjexpeditions.com. He also leads expeditions to the Libyan Desert.

I am grateful, too, for the generous assistance of Kurt Mayer, son of the Viennese cinematographer Rudi Mayer who filmed Almasy's 1929 expedition to East Africa and Sudan and allowed me to reproduce some stills from his father's film. Kurt came across his father's long-forgotten silent footage in a desk drawer in 1996 and refashioned it into an award-winning, hour-long TV documentary, *Durch Afrika im Automobil*. Later, he wrote and directed *Treacherous Sands*, a TV documentary on Almasy's life. Both are available via <u>kurtmayerfilm@chello.at</u>.

I was also given unstinted help by Peter Clayton, son of the Desert Survey topographer Patrick Clayton, who figures largely in these pages. Clayton gave me copies of some of the most interesting of the otherwise unobtainable documents. He also gave me clearance to use a number of unique photographs from his father's collection.

I must also mention here my research assistant, translator and interpreter, Sara Molnar, who guided me through the otherwise impenetrable linguistic and cultural thickets of her native Hungary. She also helped me track down the remarkable story of Jeno Fuchs which, like the Holocaust altogether, seems to be another subject Hungarians nowadays do not like to talk about.

Thanks are also due to Stephen Bagnold, son of the remarkable desert pioneer, self-taught polymath and founder of the wartime Long Range Desert Group, Major (later Brigadier) Ralph Bagnold; to the Hungarian-American scholar Steven Totosy de Zepetnek; to Peter Steigerwald, Bjoern Schipper and Gabriel Hampel, all three of the Frobenius Institute, Goethe University, Frankfurt; to Rachel Osterreicher-Bernheim, of the Raoul Wallenberg Committee of the United States; to Laszlone Kis of the Vas County Archive; and to Bob Slater, Geoff Sanford, Kate Wacz, Carla Singer, Andras Hamori, Gloria Bishop,

John Rubinstein and Eva Rubinstein, Tony Hart, Gina Pietralunga, Jolyon Halse, David Greenway, Logan Lewis-Proudlook and Jean Howard.

Paphos, Cyprus, January 2004

Sources

Prologue

p. 1 Abdin Palace in the 50s and Farouk's lifestyle, Stadiem, *Too Rich*, p. 5 et seq.

p. 4 'stiff as a statue', Bagnold, *Wind, Sand and War*, p. 156

p. 5 'If you don't believe me', Bagnold to Jean Howard, 2/4/78, Churchill Archives, Bagnold Papers, BGND C31

p. 6 'alone and neglected', Howard to Bagnold, 6/12/78, ibid.

p. 6 'a Nazi but a sportsman', *Geographical Journal*, vol. 117, June 1951

p. 7 'It is this utter denigration', Hurka, 'Philosophy, Morality and *The English Patient*', *Queen's Quarterly*, Ottawa, Spring 1997

p. 8 'a committed Nazi collaborator', Salett, *Washington Post*, CO1, 12/4/96

p. 8 'but an interpretation', interview quoted in Steven Totosy de Zepetnek, *CLC Website Journal*, 1.4, December 1999

Chapter 1

I am indebted to the staff of the Szombatheley Episcopal Archives and the Vas County Archives of Almasys for their assistance in turning up photographs and documents relating to Almasy's early life and family background including his parents' divorce, his grandfather's will, etc.

p. 13 Noble but untitled Hungarians, Steven Totosy de Zepet-nek, *CLC Website Journal*, 1.4, December 1999

p. 20 'a godsend', Gilbert, *A History of the Twentieth Century*, p. 310

p. 20 'a dull cataleptic trance', ibid., p. 232

p. 21 '*We wanted something good*', ibid., p. 312

p. 23 'friends of my family', Hanna Van Horne to Lady (Judith) Listowel, 27/1/86

p. 25 Bishop Mikes not Almasy's 'uncle', e-mailed information from de Zepetnek to author, 5/3/03

Chapter 2

p. 28 Janos 'surrounded by beautiful women', Victor-Mansour Semeika, interviewed by *Egyptian Mail*, 7 June 1997

p. 30 'indescribable tests', Almasy, *The Unknown Sahara* (Zboray translation), p. 3

p. 33 'unforgettable expedition', ibid., p. 4

p. 35 'no more formidable obstacle', Moorehead, *The White Nile*, p. 83

p. 36 'This consisted', Almasy, p. 34

p. 38 'The life of the Bedu', Michael Asher, *Thesiger*, p. 393

p. 38 'most perfect expression of total freedom', ibid., p. 4

p. 38 'nearer to the Creator', ibid., p. 6

p. 38 'The desert is terrible', ibid., p. 7

Chapter 3

p. 39 'nothing like these sand seas', Kennedy Shaw, *Long Range Desert Group*, p. 37

p. 41 'an imitation of Hell', ibid., p. 42

p. 41 'one of the most lovely things', ibid., p. 83

p. 44 'At the end of an hour', Mason, *The Paradise of Fools*, p. 43

p. 45 'I increased speed', Bagnold, *Libyan Sands*, pp. 157–8

p. 46 'An extraordinarily powerful impulse', ibid., p. 80

p. 46 'pleasure, interest and excitement', Bagnold, p. 326

While Bagnold describes his desert-driving techniques and innovations in his memoirs, *Sand, Wind and War* and *Libyan Sands*, Almasy is not at all informative on such matters in *The Unknown Sahara* and subsequent writings.

Chapter 4

The description of Almasy's journey with Lichtenstein along the Forty Days Road is of necessity drawn almost entirely from his original account in *Az Ismeretlen Szahara* (*The Unknown Sahara*). If Lichtenstein wrote his own account, corroborative or otherwise, it has not survived. While there is no reason to doubt the overall truthfulness of Almasy's version, it does include one or two incidents which he withheld from his more sober account for the more knowledgeable readers of the *Sudan Notes and Records* (vol. XIII, 1930). For instance, he makes no mention of encountering a fifteen-strong band of camel raiders at Selima and paying them to carry his petrol to a dump two days' march away, they leaving their rifles with him as 'surety'.

p. 48 'slaves, male and female', quoted in Bagnold, *Libyan Sands*, p. 135

p. 51 'a wonder of nature', Almasy, *The Unknown Sahara*, p. 14

p. 51 'a hard-mouthed old harridan', Mason, *The Paradise of Fools*, p. 64

p. 53 'a dreadful urge to flee', Almasy, p. 29

p. 54 'like a grenade', ibid., p. 30

p. 55 'The prayers at night', Ahmed Mohammed Hassanein Bey, diary entry, 30/4/23

p. 56 'shivers ran through my back', Almasy, p. 34

Chapter 5

The account of Gerhard Rohlfs's desert explorations is based on his 1875 publication, *Drei Monaten in der Libyischen Wuste*; Rosita Forbes's trip to Kufra is based on her 1921 publication, *The Secrets of the Sahara: Kufara*. Hassanein Bey's account is drawn from his 1925 book *The Lost Oases*.

p. 61 'find freedom', Forbes, *Appointment with Destiny*, p. 54

p. 62 'I never attempted records', Almasy, *The Unknown Sahara*, p. 2

p. 62 'No sooner', Bagnold, *Libyan Sands*, p. 328

p. 65 'a question of life and death', cited in Sykes, *Orde Wingate*, p. 74

Sources

p. 66 'No one, going forth', Orde Wingate, 'In Search of Zerzura', *Geographical Journal*, vol. 83, 1934

Chapter 6

p. 67 'His treatment of', *Geographical Journal*, vol. 71, 1933
p. 67 'his imagination took fire', ibid.
p. 68 'disappointments and rebuttals', Almasy, *The Unknown Sahara*, p. 5
p. 69 'sewn up with bootlaces', *Geographical Journal*, vol. 71, 1933
p. 70 'without any forethought', Almasy, p. 38
p. 70 'the noble tranquillity', ibid., p. 42
p. 71 'the worst flight', Clayton–East–Clayton, *The Times*, 6/7/32
p. 72 'only the slightest chance', *Geographical Journal*, vol. 71, 1933
p. 72 'we brewed a cup of tea', ibid.
p. 73 'too bad for a forced landing', ibid.

Chapter 7

My account of the Italian colonization of Libya owes much to Antonio del Boca's *Gli Italiani in Libia*.

p. 78 'the fanatic xenophobia', Almasy, *The Unknown Sahara*, p. 51
p. 78 'difficult to exaggerate', Kennedy Shaw, *Long Range Desert Group*, p. 79
p. 78 'broad-minded and clever', Almasy, p. 56

p. 79 'warm emotions', ibid., p. 58

p. 79 'quite possibly Zerzura', *The Times*, 6/7/42

p. 79 'Old man Wadi has beaten us!', *Geographical Journal*, vol. 71, 1933

p. 80 'We consider it certain', ibid.

p. 80 'traitors and spies', *The Times*, 31/1/31

p. 81 'the natural consequence', ibid., 17/9/31

p. 82 'At nine in the evening', Rahman diary quoted in Almasy, p. 78

p. 83 'no need for this', ibid., p. 76

p. 83 'The women's feet', Peter Clayton, *Desert Explorer*, p. 38; report to Desert Surveys 26/4/31, PRO FO 371/15433

p. 84 'After a great struggle', Bagnold, *Libyan Sands*, p. 249

p. 84 'The total number', letter to *The Times*, 25/5/31

p. 85 'a dubious person', Most Confidential report, Kufra to HQ Benghazi, 23/4/33, quoted in Clayton, p. 67

Chapter 8

p. 86 Prince Kemal's life and death, Samir Raafat, 'Palaces on the Nile', *Cairo Times*, 25/12/97

p. 88 Sir Robert's death, *The Times*, 15/9/32

p. 88 'carrying on my husband's work', *News Chronicle*, 13/2/33

p. 89 'immediately detected his homosexual tendencies', Clayton, *Desert Explorer*, p. 63

p. 90 'a little optimism and a Ford', *The Times*, 16/9/33

p. 92 'very little difficulty', ibid.

p. 93 'narrowed down the Zerzura problem', ibid.

p. 93 Inquest evidence, *The Times* and *Daily Express*, 19/3/33

p. 94 'difficult to explain', *Flight* magazine, 21/9/33

Chapter 9

p. 96 'although primitive in character', Ahmed Mohammed Hassanein Bey, diary entry, 30/4/23

p. 98 'surpassing any previously known', Almasy, *The Unknown Sahara*, p. 6

p. 98 'almost futuristic', ibid., p. 103

p. 99 'could not suppress their wonder', ibid.

p. 100 'the dear professor', ibid., p. 6

p. 100 'especially fortunate', Rohtert, *Libyische Felsbilder*, p. 2

p. 100 'the most beautiful finds', ibid.

Chapter 10

p. 102 'I prefer to think', Bagnold, *Libyan Sands*, p. 344

p. 103 'a withered old man', Churchill Archives, Bagnold Papers, BGND B.18

p. 103 Abd el Malik's story, ibid.

p. 105 'correct in every detail', ibid.

p. 106 'a serious discrepancy', ibid.

p. 106 'not a single stone tool', Almasy, *The Unknown Sahara*, p. 74

p. 106 'truly seen', ibid.

p. 106 'The Last of the Zerzura Legend', *Geographical Journal*, vol. 89, 1937

p. 107 'as long as any part', Bagnold, *Libyan Sands*, p. 347

Chapter 11

p. 108 'an agent of the complex English', Cantalupo to MFA, Rome, ASMAE 1/10/32

p. 109 'not tourist information', ibid.

p. 110 'three days' run', Kennedy Shaw, *Long Range Desert Group*, pp. 13, 14

p. 110 'eccentric and somewhat unpleasant', PRO FO 371/ 18034 – 19099

p. 111 'likeable and amusing', Bagnold to Jean Howard, 2/4/78, Churchill Archives, Bagnold Papers, BGND C31

p. 111 'getting very tired', PRO FO 371/18034, Cairo Chancery to FO 17/2/34

p. 111 'This is interesting', ibid.

p. 111 'rather a mystery man', ibid.

p. 112 'nothing definitely sinister', ibid.

p. 112 'von der Esch was a German spy', Kennedy Shaw, p. 169

p. 113 'It is certain', Rawlinson, *History of Herodotus*, pp. 426–7

p. 114 British were behind', Cantalupo to MFA, Rome, 1/10/32 ASMAE

p. 115 'eyewash', PRO FO 371/17035

p. 115 'be careful', RGS, Kennedy Shaw Papers, Fabri to HQ Benghazi, 23/4/32

p. 115 Easy access to Nile Valley, ASMAE, Pagliano to Fgn Min., Rome, 9/6/33

p. 115 'dangerously near', PRO, FO 371/17035, Maurice Peterson, 23/6/33

p. 116 'essential to put a check', PRO, CAB 51/1, COS 320, 26/1/34

p. 116 'Fashoda type of threat', PRO, FO 371/1/17035, Peterson 6/12/33

p. 117 ' "do his bit" for British', *Magyarorszag*, quoted in MAI Posizione 150/28, 26/10/35 cited in Kelly, *The Hunt for Zerzura*

p. 117 'an instrument of the English', MAI Posizione 150/28, Fgn Min. to Min. of Colonies 28/11/35, cited in Kelly, p. 123

p. 118 'strongly opposed', PRO FO 371/19099, Lampson to FO 20/12/35

p. 118 'light air-wheels', ibid., Symes to Lampson, 1/12/35

p. 118 'Sooner or later', Henderson to Chamberlain 11/1/38, PRO FO 371/21997

p. 119 'a disaster for Egypt', ibid.

p. 119 'how many British regiments?', ibid.

p. 120 'it was already known', Elizabeth Salett, *Washington Post*, 4/12/96

Chapter 12

p. 122 'keen and rather bird-like', Mason, *The Paradise of Fools*, p. 106

p. 123 'It may be assumed', Almasy, *The Unknown Sahara*, p. 109

p. 124 'violently anti-British', Yapp (ed.), *The Diaries of Sir Miles Lampson*, p. 544

p. 125 'terribly sorry for the Fuehrer', Lovell, *The Mitford Girls*, p. 173

Sources

p. 128 'Hitler was her one god', Pryce-Jones, *Unity Mitford: A Quest*, p. 143

p. 128 'a brief love affair', Lovell, p. 270

p. 129 'a camouflaged Jew', Pryce-Jones, p. 143

p. 129 'the Danish cow', ibid.

p. 129 'Out with the Jews!', Lovell, p. 188

The Entholt–Almasy correspondence, as stated in the text, derives from unsorted, uncatalogued letters found by Kurt Mayer at Castle Bernstein in 1995 and believed by the author, on empirical evidence, to be authentic.

Chapter 13

p. 135 Unity Mitford's hospitalization and return – details in Lovell, *The Mitford Girls* and Pryce-Jones, *Unity Mitford*

p. 137 'a tall, distinguished-looking man', Ritter, *Deckname Dr Rantzau*, p. 262

p. 138 'a fantastic idea', ibid.

p. 138 'Almasy was sure', ibid., p. 263

p. 139 'Then he stared into space', Almasy, *With Rommel's Army in Libya*, introduction by Dr Janos Kubassek, p. x

Chapter 14

p. 142 'a man of vision', Bagnold, *Libyan Sands*, p. 286

p. 142 'What a man', Bagnold, *Sand, Wind and War*, p. 125

p. 144 'like ducks to water', ibid., p. 219

p. 145 'We could not travel', Bagnold, IWM Sound Archive 9862/3

p. 146 'got the full attention', Peter Clayton, *Desert Explorer*, p. 153

p. 146 'very good to us', ibid., p. 153

p. 146 'a master-stroke', *Popolo d'Italia*, 18/10/41

p. 147 'the whole credit', Clayton, p. 147

p. 147 'masterly', 'When the patrol', ibid., pp. 148–9

p. 148 'We are *in extremis*', Kennedy Shaw, *Long Range Desert Group*, p. 77

Chapter 15

The account in this and subsequent chapters of the seesawing 1940–43 North African campaign is based on official historical sources such as I. S. O. Playfair's *History of the Second World War* and later assessments of the desert war, including Bierman and Smith's *Alamein: War Without Hate*.

p. 151 'with but not for', Ritter, *Deckname Dr Rantzau*, p. 396

p. 152 'a man of great importance', KV 2/87, dated 29/9/41

p. 155 'Everything in order', GCCS File no. 5798, Ritter to Hamburg 27/5/41

p. 157 'I had myself to blame', Ritter, p. 450

p. 158 'We have reliable information', IWM, LRDG 4/5, Kennedy Shaw Papers, FBIN to Prendergast, 14/11/41

p. 158 'an *ersatz* Bagnold', Kennedy Shaw, *Long Range Desert Group*, p. 168

Sources

Chapter 16

p. 160 'At noon I arrive', Almasy, *With Rommel's Army in Libya*, p. 46

p. 161 'I can tell', ibid., p. 46

p. 162 'My officer candidate', ibid., pp. 47–8

p. 162 'The plane comes', ibid., p. 56

p. 164 'I can hardly wait', ibid., p. 64

p. 165 Captured documents re Almasy Commando, GSI(s) 8th Army to LRDG HQ, 5/6/42, Lloyd-Owen Papers, IWM

Chapter 17

p. 169 'I had noticed', Mrs Jean Howard, in conversation with the author, October 2002

p. 169 'this man must be caught', interview with Kurt Mayer, September 1999

p. 170 'officer candidate', Almasy, *With Rommel's Army in Libya*, p. 46 et seq.

p. 170 'not fit to travel', GSI(s) 8th Army to LRDG HQ, 5/6/42, Lloyd-Owen Papers, IWM

p. 171 'We must go via Kufra!' et seq., ibid. Almasy, Operation Salam diary (in Lloyd-Owen Papers, ibid.)

Sources

Chapter 18

p. 185 'it does not seem necessary', Almasy, Operation Salam diary, p. 13

p. 186 'This is <u>not</u> el Aqaba', ibid., p. 14

p. 187 'We have to get out', ibid.

p. 187 'No shooting', ibid., p. 16

p. 188 'Good job', ibid., p. 17

p. 188 'a good effort', Kennedy Shaw, *Long Range Desert Group*, p. 171

p. 190 'out of the *Thousand and One Nights*, Sadat, *Revolt on the Nile*, p. 47

p. 192 'riotous living', PRO WO 208/1561, Middle East Security Survey 14/10/42

Chapter 19

p. 194 'his old buddy', Buchheit, *The German Secret Service*, quoted in Clayton, *Desert Explorer*, p. 156

p. 194 'The remarks about Pat', ibid., p. 158

p. 195 'many strange references', ibid., p. 162

p. 197 'Our three vehicles', Almasy, *With Rommel's Army in Libya*, p. 97

p. 198 'Over many years', ibid., p. 98

p. 198 'The words of the gospel', ibid., p. 79

p. 199 'Haj Taher's house', ibid., p. 86

p. 199 'In Egypt did I meet', ibid., p. 90

p. 200 'Rommel is a muscular', ibid., p. 60

p. 200 'I can somehow comprehend', ibid., p. 68

Chapter 20

The circumstances of Hungary's Jewish minority before and during the Nazi occupation, and details of Raoul Wallenberg's remarkable rescue efforts, are drawn from authoritative historical sources such as Randolph Braham's *The Destruction of Hungarian Jewry* (New York, 1963), Per Anger's *With Wallenberg in Budapest* (Stockholm, 1979), Lars Berg's *What Happened in Budapest* (Stockholm, 1949), and personal reminiscences as published in my book, *Righteous Gentile*.

p. 209 'this solution', quoted in Bierman, *Righteous Gentile*, p. 76

p. 211 Re 'Arkos Antal', Kubassek, *A Szahara Buvoleteben*, pp. 217–18

p. 213 'physically unimposing', *Olympika: The International Journal of Olympic Studies*, vol. V, 1996, pp. 151–8

p. 214 'the greatest masters of the sabre', *Swedish Olympic Report*, 1912, quoted on internet website jewsinsport.org

Chapter 21

p. 222 'I wish I hadn't', quoted in Pryce-Jones, *Unity Mitford*, p. 143

p. 222 'Horrible platitudes!', ibid., p. 242

p. 222 'half-crying with fear', ibid.

p. 223 'One had to try to save the castle' et seq., Janos Almasy, *The Occupation of Bernstein* (unpublished manuscript)

Chapter 22

p. 232 Rakosi's phone call to People's Court, etc., Kubassek, *A Szahara Buvoleteben*, p. 235

p. 232 Almasy's deposition and other People's Court trial details, Hungarian National Archives, file xxv 1.a N63501/1946

p. 233 Fuchs's Iron Cross award, Gyorgy Szilagyi, 'Yellow Armband and Iron Cross', *Hungarian Olympic Bulletin*, no. 45, 1993. (This unusual award is also mentioned in the *Hungarian Olympic Lexicon*, Budapest, 2000, and *Hungarian Olympic Champions: 1896–1996*, Budapest, 2000.)

Chapter 23

p. 238 Tea with Hitler, et al., Valderano, *The Owl and the Pussycat*, Minerva Press, London, 1988, p. 30

p. 238 Valderano's schooling etc., Old Stoics' Register, Stowe School, Buckinghamshire 2001

p. 241 Almasy's escape, ibid., pp. 125–8, and Valderano interview with Kubassek, August 1999

Chapter 24

p. 244 'no money at all', Waring/Valderano interviewed for TV documentary *Treacherous Sands* by Kurt Mayer, 1999

p. 245 Almasy medical details, cited by Kubassek in *A Szahara Buvoleteben*, p. 258

p. 246 Almasy funeral details, ibid., p. 259

p. 247 'In the infinity of the desert', Almasy, *The Unknown Sahara*, p. 7

Bibliography

Almasy, Laszlo, *The Unknown Sahara (Az Ismeretlen Szahara)*, Franklin, Budapest, 1934; English trans. Andras Zboray, 2000, *www.fjexpeditions.com*

——*Récentes Explorations dans le Désert Libyque (1932–36)*, Royal Geographical Society of Egypt, Cairo, 1936

——*With Rommel's Army in Libya (Rommel seregenel Libyaban)*, Arrow Press, Budapest, 1934; reprinted Denes Natur Muhely, Budapest, 1999; English trans. Gabriel Francis Hoerchler

——*Schwimmer in der Wuste* (ed. and introd. Raoul Schrott and Michael Farin), DTV, Munich, 2001

Asher, Michael, *In Search of the Forty Days Road*, Penguin, London, 1986

——*Thesiger*, Viking, London, 1994

Bagnold, Ralph A., *Sand, Wind and War: Memoirs of a Desert Explorer*, University of Arizona Press, Tucson, 1990

——*Libyan Sands: Travels in a Dead World*, Hodder & Stoughton, London, 1935

Behrend, Hans-Otto, *Rommel's Intelligence in the Desert Campaign*, William Kimber, London, 1985

Bierman, John, *Righteous Gentile*, Viking, London, 1981; rev. edn. 1995

Bierman, John, and Smith, Colin, *Alamein: War Without Hate*, Viking, London, 2002

——*Fire in the Night*, Macmillan, London, 1999

Buchheit, Gerd (trans. Helga Wocherl), *The German Secret Service*, Paul List, Munich, 1966

Clayton, Peter, *Desert Explorer*, Zerzura Press, Cargreen, Cornwall, 1998

Cooper, Artemis, *Cairo in the War, 1939–45*, Penguin, London, 1995

Del Boca, A., *Gli Italiani in Libia, dal Fascismo a Ghedafi*, Editore Latia, Rome, 1998

Eppler, Johann, *Operation Condor: Rommel's Spy*, Futura, London, 1978

Forbes, Rosita, *The Secrets of the Sahara: Kufara*, Cassell, London, 1921

——*Appointment with Destiny*, Cassell, London, 1946

Gilbert, Martin, *A History of the Twentieth Century*, vol. 1, HarperCollins, London, 1997

Gordon, John W., *The Other Desert War*, Greenwood Press, Westport, Conn., 1987

Hassanein, Ahmed, Mohammed, *The Lost Oases*, Thornton-Butterworth, London, 1925

Hinsley, F. H., and Stripp, Alan (eds), *Code Breakers: The Inside Story of Bletchley Park*, OUP, Oxford, 1993

Hollriegel, Arnold (Richard Bermann), *Zerzura: Die Oase der kleinen Voegel*, Orell Fussli Verlag, Zurich, 1938

Kelly, Saul, *The Hunt for Zerzura*, John Murray, London, 2002

Kennedy Shaw, W. B., *Long Range Desert Group*, Collins, London, 1945

Kubassek, Janos, *A Szahara Buvoleteben*, Panorama, Budapest, 2002

Lovell, Mary S., *The Mitford Girls*, Little, Brown, London, 2001

Macartney, M. A., *October Fifteenth: A History of Modern Hungary 1929–1945*, 2 vols, Edinburgh University Press, 1961

Mason, Michael, *The Paradise of Fools*, Hodder & Stoughton, London, 1936

Molwar, M. (trans. A. J. Pomerans), *From Bela Kun to Janos Kadar: Seventy Years of Hungarian Communism*, Berg, London, 1990

Moorehead, Alan, *The White Nile*, Hamish Hamilton, London, 1972

Playfair, I. S. O., *History of the Second World War: The Mediterranean and the Middle East*, HMSO, London, 1966

Pryce-Jones, David, *Unity Mitford: A Quest*, Weidenfeld & Nicolson, London, 1972

Rawlinson, G. M. (ed.), *History of Herodotus*, vol. 2, John Murray, London, 1888

Ritter, N., *Deckname Dr Rantzau*, Hoffmann & Campe Verlag, Hamburg, 1972

Robertson, E., *Mussolini as Empire Builder: Europe and Africa, 1932–36*, Macmillan, London, 1977

Rohlfs, Gerhard, *Drei Monaten in der Libyischen Wuste*, Theodor Fischer, Cassel, 1875

Rohtert, Hans, *Libyische Felsbilder*, L. C. Wittich Verlag, Darmstadt, 1952

Sadat, Anwar, *Revolt on the Nile*, Allan Wingate, London, 1957

Sansom, A. E. W., *I Spied Spies*, Harrap, London, 1965

Stadiem, William, *Too Rich: The High Life and Tragic Death of King Farouk*, Carroll & Graf, New York, 1991

Sykes, Christopher, *Orde Wingate*, Collins, London, 1959

Thompson, Julian, *War Behind Enemy Lines*, IWM/Sidgwick & Jackson, London, 1988

Yapp, M. E. (ed.), *The Diaries of Sir Miles Lampson*, OUP, Oxford, 1997

Index

Page numbers followed by the letter n indicate note at bottom of that page. Entry for Laszlo Almasy has been divided into chronological sections followed by two general sections – character and friendships. LA stands for Laszlo Almasy throughout.

Index